# STUDIES IN PRICING

# STUDIES IN PRICING

P. W. S. Andrews
and
Elizabeth Brunner

*First published 1975 by*
THE MACMILLAN PRESS LTD
*London and Basingstoke*
*Associated companies in New York*
*Dublin Melbourne Johannesburg and Madras*

ISBN 978-1-349-02717-0     ISBN 978-1-349-02715-6 (eBook)
DOI 10.1007/978-1-349-02715-6

*Typeset in Great Britain by*
PREFACE LTD.
*Salisbury, Wiltshire*

To Mary Andrews

# Contents

# Preface

This book is composed of essays on the theory and practice of pricing. Before Philip Andrews's death in 1971 we were thinking of such a book, but it has been left to me to put it together.

The first two essays are a pair of lectures. They were given originally, the first by Andrews and the second by myself, at the University of Paris in 1965 and the French versions were published shortly afterwards.* Slightly different versions were then given at the University of Harvard in 1966, and it is these which are published here. The first, on the crisis in micro-economic theory, was written solely by Andrews and, if my memory is right, with very little assistance from me. It expresses the sort of worries about traditional economic theory which are given at greater length and with more specific references in his book *On Competition in Economic Theory* (Macmillan, 1964). It gives the critical reasons why Andrews felt the need to develop a new approach to the theory of the firm.

The second essay is my own attempt to put Andrews's theory positively in economists' traditional terms so that it can more easily be grasped by those trained in static marginalist equilibrium economics. Andrews was not altogether sympathetic to the attempt to put new wine in old bottles, and he said, reasonably, that if his theory could have been expressed at chapter length he would not have written a book. The reader must be aware, therefore, that the 'model' form of Andrews's theory presented in Chapter 2 is no substitute for the richness of detail and argument in his *Manufacturing Business* (Macmillan, 1949). But, in so far as his theory can be presented at this length, he himself approved of this chapter. Although the actual writing was mine, he gave me very great help in the preparation of the paper.

The third essay is designed to provide a bridge between the essays on the theory of the firm and the two industrial studies included here. The essay harks back to that by Andrews on 'Industrial Analysis in Economics, with special reference to Marshall' in *Oxford Studies in the Price*

---

*P. W. S. Andrews, 'La Théorie Micro-Économique en État de Crise', *Revue d'Économie Politique*, 1966; E. Brunner, 'Prix Concurrentiels, Coûts Normaux, et Stabilité de la Branche', *Revue d'Économie Politique*, 1967.

*Mechanism*, edited by T. Wilson and P. W. S. Andrews (Oxford: Clarendon Press, 1951). I felt that that had been pigeonholed too easily as relating only to Marshall instead of to Andrew's own system of thought. I suggested to Andrews that we should have another look at the subject, and he agreed enthusiastically, but we did not have the opportunity to do this work jointly. This essay was in fact written while I was Visiting Professor for the fall semester 1974 in the Department of Economics, Case Western Reserve University, Cleveland. I am grateful to all my colleagues there, for the friendly and stimulating atmosphere in which to work and for their discussion of this as a seminar paper. My debt to Professor Bela Gold is deeper, and is both particular and general. He helped me immeasurably both by reading and commenting on drafts of this paper, and by our general discussions in this area. The faults that remain are due to my obstinacy.

The two industrial studies included here were each undertaken for specific extraneous reasons: in the one case we were asked to help a manufacturers' association defend its agreement in the Restrictive Practices Court, and in the other we were asked by the directorate of the Building Research Station to help its staff experience more personal research methods than might otherwise be open to them. The two industries are in many ways dissimilar: the water-tube boilermakers are relatively few, and they face a single dominant customer in the Central Electricity Generating Board, so one might see it as a classical oligopoly/oligopsony confrontation, with the manufacturers colluding on price in a research-based industry with a technologically advanced and rapidly changing product. The building industry, on the other hand, is a very widespread industry, with many firms, much more obviously competitive, with a much more traditional product and processes. Both have in common, however, that the method of obtaining work is primarily through tenders, and therefore they have common problems in lumpiness of work, balance of operations, favoured customer relationships, susceptibility to Government influence on the demand from public authorities, and so on.

As regards Andrews's proof of evidence in the case of the Water Tube Boilermakers' Association, my memory is that I helped him in collecting material and compiling the tables, but that the actual writing of the proof was his own work entirely. Andrews was the witness, not I; since he was to be examined on his proof, he felt he had to be able to stand by every word, and he could only do that if they were his own words. Nevertheless, when I went back to the transcripts of the hearing, I noticed that counsel had introduced the proof as our joint work. I certainly had the fun of sitting through the whole case, observing the work of the Court, and myself working day by day with counsel, solicitors and witnesses. I have drawn on my own observations in writing the introductory note. I am indebted to Mr Jeremy Lever, one of the counsel in the case, for reading a draft of this and for his help in relation to legal aspects of the Water Tube Boilermakers case, but the opinions expressed are, of course, my own.

The provenance of the long essay on the building industry is described in the introduction to the paper itself. When it came to writing up the results, Andrews and I planned the outline together and then simply divided the work, so that he wrote the first half of the original draft and I wrote the second half. We then sent our joint effort to all our colleagues for comment, and some commented very fully. I then myself rewrote the whole report, taking account of all these comments and producing what I thought was a finished manuscript. Andrews did not like this and therefore undertook to rewrite it. He got a long way on with this task, greatly expanding the first half of the manuscript, and then got overtaken by events and abandoned the work. I have now tried once more to make a whole of it. I acknowledge gratefully the help of our colleagues in the lively discussions in the seminar in which they all took part, and in the comments they made on the earlier draft of this paper. But the long delay in presenting this report makes it especially desirable to absolve our colleagues from responsibility for any deficiencies. So also must Andrews be absolved; it will be obvious to those who know his work that he had a major hand in the first three-and-a-half sections, but the responsibility for the more summary treatment of the last one-and-a-half sections, and the balance, or lack of balance, of the final report, is mine alone.

It remains for me to make a general disclaimer. I take responsibility for all of these essays. If there is a mistake, it is mine. The absence of the first-rate technical mind which did not let mistakes pass is only one of the reasons for which I miss my collaborator. It did not seem appropriate to ask any other colleague to read these essays, with the exception of the one I wrote most recently at Case Western Reserve University.

E. B.

*University of Lancaster*
*January 1975*

# 1 The Crisis in Micro-economic Theory[*]

## INTRODUCTION

Before getting into details, I want to say something about my objective and the general methodological background to it. This lecture is no mere revisionist exercise, but a call to reform the micro-economic theory which is the central core of economic analysis. It is no accident that my views have developed in course of trying to handle oligopoly in a systematic fashion. In all sophisticated writings today, one will find recognition that oligopoly is a prevalent industrial situation, and it therefore needs to be brought squarely within the main body of economic analysis. At the same time, as we all know, our marginalist equilibrium analysis cannot handle stable oligopoly situations in terms of the independent competition of individual businesses.

In the interest of the training of our students in the marginalist methodology, we sweep all this under the carpet during the formative stages. Remember the incantatory phrases with which the greatest modern introductory text lulls the student into taking it on trust that, some way or another, everything in the oligopolies of real life will work out in terms of the analysis which he has been so thoroughly trained to apply to the theoretical cases of competition and monopoly. And at more advanced levels, this promise seems to be fulfilled in two ways. First, there are discussions of how workable-competition conditions with easy entry, not very adequately analysed, might induce behaviour of the competitive pattern. Second, and more prevalently latterly, you may pay your money and take your choice on the monopoly side of analysis, between monopolistic collusion and the categorical monopoly which is the only analytical classification which can possibly fit the behaviourist, non-maximising, satisficing, management-oriented, and suchlike, ways of evading economic analysis which have recently become most popular. I shall have something more to say about all this later, but, to justify my language meanwhile, may I note that it is surely an evasion of economic

*Given as a lecture at Harvard University, March 1966.

analysis not to be able to handle the response of entities to their economic environment; and it is not surprising that we should hear so much about problems of aggregation and disaggregation now that economists are rightly concerned with the interactions between macro-economic policy and micro-economic behaviour.

Be all this as it may, what began as an attempt to handle oligopolies has led me to question the marginalist equilibrium analysis of consumers', as well as of producers', situations. I am, then, attacking that system of analysis which postulates the equilibrium of entities, be they individual firms or consumers, as the condition for the stability of aggregates; the system under which MR equals MC and AR is not less than AC in the long run. Since I argue that we must give up all this in order to avoid serious errors of analysis, I deny that this is merely destructive, and submit an alternative plea of creative destruction. For it *is* a creative scientific task to eliminate serious error; and it is worthwhile concentrating on it while we are at it.

Because I look to the liberation of thought which might be generated by full recognition of the cumulative defects of orthodox theory, and because I would not willingly play any part in the too-rapid development of any new straight-jacket, I would not turn aside to answer our usual evasive analgesic question, 'What would you put in its place?', even if there were time to do so. I regard that question as irrelevant to my task today, and have worked out a good deal of an alternative system which is free from the errors with which I charge orthodox marginalist methodology. Both my own theoretical system and the criticisms which I present today have of course a common origin in a long period of immersion in the details of business affairs to which our empirical researches and our graduate teaching have led us. This chapter, together with the publication of my *On Competition in Economic Theory*, marks my having become persuaded that, however distasteful criticism may be, it is necessary to make this frontal attack on marginalist equilibrium methodology. I think this to be necessary, not only so that alternative analyses may be fairly considered, but also so that the able young men whom we are now so successful in recruiting shall see that our science is indeed open to new work in the face of reality. Too often, theoretical criteria imply the dissolving away of the real situations which we theorists leave to lesser mortals to grapple with.

I make no regretful bow in the direction of welfare economics, and am unmoved by appeals to the grand simplicity of marginalism as a training tool which enables freshmen to criticise the real world in the abstract, while they are still wet behind the ears. If shorn of basic applicability, I doubt if the intellectual discipline of that hieromancy would prove superior to that of astrology. I am more moved by the thought of the several fine mathematicians whom we have inveigled into our science and given the freedom of our craft, subject only to the condition that their analyses always end with MR equals MC, Pareto optima *et al.* I have hopes that the analyses of aggregates under non-micro-equilibrium conditions may be more stimulating to genuine mathematical creativity.

## HISTORICAL BACKGROUND

I turn from these shocking remarks to some brief history – in particular as a reminder that non-micro-equilibrium analysis has a classical ancestry, and that micro-equilibrium economics is not so old. People who were still alive when I started economics could remember the marginalist system achieving its dominant position. Only the principle of substitution and of the minimisation of alternative costs may be said to go back to the grass-roots of economics, and, far from challenging that, I appeal to it for one of my major criticisms of marginalist orthodoxy. In brief, the older supply and demand approach to the stability of individual industrial markets certainly did not predicate that firms and consumers were in individual equilibrium even in conditions of long-run stability.

Micro-equilibrium method came in with the development of consumer demand theory. The power with which that cleared up ancient conundra, such as the paradox of value, led to the extension of the method, particularly in the hands of the great continental European schools of economics, of which the definitive text is perhaps to be found in the work of Walras. In this, and on the basis of the postulated equilibrium of consumer- and producer-entities, was worked out the grand design of the neo-classical analysis of competition.

I see this development as a major source of error for the micro-economic and industrial analyses which are so important to us. But I do not traduce the analysis of a *system* of competition for the larger-scale, macro, purposes for which it was originally used and by which economists achieved understanding of the broad working of the private-enterprise pricing system, and of the broad system of income distribution resulting from that. At this high level of analysis, I suggest that the theory had a validity which is not impugned by the narrower-focus criticism to which it was later subjected; what was involved was the interconnexion between prices at different points of the economic system. 'Firms' and 'consumers' are but terms in the broader analysis, marking, it may be said, nodes at which is exhibited the balancing of the larger forces at work in society. There, was generated that vision of the economic system which has become fragmented by later development of analysis in the interest of smaller-scale realism – except in so far as the vision has misleadingly been transferred out of real time to the celestial kingdom of the welfare schools.

We know, of course, what happened to the positive theory – partly, indeed, under the influence of the development of welfare analysis by the Cambridge, England, School (which, for reasons to become apparent, I refrain from calling Marshallian): attention was concentrated on the equilibria of individual industries in terms of the postulated equilibria of the firms within them. The, from this point of view, careless, realism of the older supply and demand analysis could not be sustained. The condition that firms be in equilibrium ruled out the more important manifestations of the increasing returns which had earlier been ascribed to whole competitive industries.

The puzzle was that such increasing-returns industries did exhibit in practice the kind of normal stability which had been translated into the competitive industrial equilibrium, and that, in such stability, one also found what I have characterised as the compatibility of costs and prices, which itself had been mirrored in the theoretical terms of the cost/profit equilibria of competition analysis. How could one reconcile these stigmata of competitive industries with decreasing costs at the level of the firm?

It was the great positive achievement of Edward Chamberlin to get such a compatibility of prices and costs with stable conditions for the firm and for the industrial group, in his large-group analysis, in the simplified model in which he presented it most fully. This achievement ceased to be valued, even by its author, under the influence of the recognition of the importance of small-group oligopolies, for which neither Chamberlin's nor any other orthodox-base analyses have ever been able to cater (and where even Chamberlin finally took refuge in collusion as the explanation of the kind of stability found in practice). It is, nevertheless, of interest that there is such a strong propensity to preserve the falling demand curves for the individual firm, even in the analysis of oligopoly where, as I have indicated, they lack rigorous justification. What I shall later have to say in criticism of these same kinds of demand curves, whether for large-group or for small-group analysis, must not obscure the achievement of Professor Chamberlin in terms of the questions which were holding up the development of economics at the time when he created his analysis. (Nor should one minimise, on the grounds of my criticism of the thereafter-orthodox treatment of advertising, Chamberlin's great liberating achievement in causing economists to begin to look at advertising as something which they might handle analytically, whatever the demerits of his selling-cost approach.)

Before finally turning to my detailed criticisms of marginalist equilibrium theory, I should observe that Marshall himself, pioneer though he had been in the development of the relevant consumer demand theory, is not to be classified as a micro-equilibrium theorist so far as the firm is concerned, and his device of the 'representative' firm is as much a sign that he, excellent mathematician though he was, refused to take this step into the modern orthodoxy as it is a sign that he was defeated by positive analysis of the individual firm's situation in what he regarded as competitive industry. For this reason, the genealogical chart of modern economics at the end of Professor Samuelson's *Economics* is mistaken in running through Marshall — the line of descent should go through Menger and Walras, who do not appear in the family tree, and Marshall should be shown as standing eccentrically but warningly on one side. In this sense, Marshall, as I have said, was not a Marshallian according to our usual classification; and I was glad to get Robertson eventually to admit this in a rather grudging fashion, though not specifically to revoke the false identification of the representative firm with Pigou's 'equilibrium' firm whose authority had misled so many of us during the famous controversy of the twenties.

## THE CASE FOR REFORM

But I do not need to appeal to Marshall to make my first major point of positive criticism, for his authority is of doutful value so far as consumer equilibrium conditions are concerned, and in other detailed matters as well. Besides my point is a matter of sheer logic, at which I have already hinted rather strongly: our basic orthodox postulate of the atomistic equilibrium of entities has no grand necessity about it. Leaving consumers on one side, I shall put my point in terms of firms: clearly, to have a steady supply from an industrial group as a whole does not entail that all firms necessarily have to cover their costs.

Turning from logic to reality, we know very well that there *are* industries where it is regularly the case that a substantial part of the total output is produced at a loss, and still more at a less than normal profit. Even the long-run theory of the stability of such an industry should, surely, presume this state of affairs rather than deny it by force of prior assumption. In many Western countries, one example is retail trade, probably because of its easy-entry, easy-exit conditions. It certainly is paradoxical, even though it is to be understood in the light of our ingrained methodology, that economists should so readily use arguments that assume that prices *have* to cover the costs of the marginal, least-efficient, firms. Professional literature on restrictive practices, moreover, is littered with examples of such casuistic phenomena. Many well-known discussions of the analysis of actual cartels will provide examples of what I have identified as the *marginal firm fallacy* inherent in orthodox analysis in consequence of our atomistic equilibrium postulate. No doubt, in such cases, the arguments to which such fallacious reasoning tends seem better than they are because we rather expect the kinds of conclusions which they reach about industries which have shut themselves out from absolute competition, but it will be a bad day for the prestige of economics when laymen who are criticised cotton on to the weak points in their condemnation. On the general tendency, I shall say only that in my *On Competition in Economic Theory* I have a good deal to say about the danger in economics of what I have called *prima facie* arguments.

The marginal firm fallacy, of course, lurks behind many expositions of the abstract virtues of perfect competition, where accounts of the efficiency which it allegedly enforces are often, by the way, bolstered by statements which are innocent of the fundamental rule that the rents of individual producers are to be written into their cost curves.

I shall return to this general error of our atomistic equilibrium methodology in connexion with other points of criticism. Immediately, I turn to the general question of product differentiation and the way we have come to handle it.

Of course, if we do not postulate full atomistic equilibrium, we need not invoke falling marginal revenues *merely* so that decreasing costs shall be compatible with the postulated equilibrium of the individual firm. There was, therefore, always an analytical gap, between the idea that differentiation connotes some kind of buyers' preferences, and the step which we took under Chamberlin, of assuming preferences which persist long run, and which are of a kind to fit the ready-made clothing of monopoly analysis.

I doubt, however, if we would so readily have accepted falling individual-firm demand curves as long-run results of buyers' preferences, were it not for our ingrained tendency to call all 'buyers' 'consumers'. Otherwise, we might not have been so ready to set up demand curves in general models, which are explained in terms of the behaviour, as we have come to picture that, of ordinary buyers of consumers' goods for their own consumption. This leads to demonstrable errors in analysis, of the kind of general validity which Chamberlin has asserted for monopolistic competition analysis. But, since this tendency is so ingrained in economists from the very first analysis of demand which we make, it is perhaps not so surprising as it should be, as a matter of sheer logic, that this mistake does not seem to have been recognised until 1949; or that it should have required so much exposure in industrial research to bring me round to it then; or, even, that my criticism has since been so generally disregarded by my colleagues! But let me make it again.

Even as a practical matter, we all know that there are important markets where goods are sold to businesses for their own use; and that even finished consumers' goods have market stages where they are sold to other businesses for resale. In such cases, the implication of our falling individual-firm demand curves is that business buyers will continue to buy a good from one source at higher prices independently of the prices at which others sell it, or would sell it. Now, this imputes irrationality to businessmen on the cost side of their calculations. If we go as far as this, we give up economic analysis altogether. In my view then, it follows that all analyses which impute falling demand curves to individual firms lack the generality which is claimed for them. It follows also that differentiation of the product does not constitute a general cause of a barrier to intra-industry competition.

Harking back to the atomistic error itself – the mere recognition of business markets would also have called into question our precious micro-equilibrium postulate. It is *that* which forces us to impute falling demand curves wherever firms' long-run costs are not increasing; yet we know that many industries selling to business customers nevertheless enjoy decreasing costs. It follows from what has already been said that we may not analyse such cases on the basis that the firms concerned *are* in an equilibrium of the kind we postulate. I hope that the damage which recognition of this does to our orthodox machinery will make us less confident that it is suitable for unquestioned use in the case of industries selling to consumers – or are we now prepared to have a different method of economic analysis in their case?

I shall not now bring in my views as to how we should analyse the effects of product differentiation, since I am restricting the discussion to errors which arise directly from our methodology, and my positive theory is not derivable only from this criticism. More narrowly, my views on consumer rationality would certainly call for persuasive argument, as distinct from the demonstrative argument which I keep to on this occasion. But a good deal of what I shall say otherwise will certainly have a bearing on the question of falling individual demand curves for the long-run analysis of firms selling consumers' goods, and this is especially the case with the question of applying our atomistic equilibrium postulate to the case of consumers, properly so called, which I next take up.

I cannot delve here into the consequences of the methodological blind spot in our normal use of demand functions, which are short run by definition, in long-run analyses which are used as guides to trends in the actual world, except to say that I have shown that there is a danger that our demand and cost curves will actually not be independent when the time dimension on the one side is so much broader than that built into the definition on the other. What I am questioning now is simply the assumption of the full static equilibrium of the individual consumer which is built into our orthodox static demand curves, whatever the time scale of the analysis.

Surely, we ought to recognise that human life, in the market-place as elsewhere, is transient and mutable. Consumers are born and die; the families which form, grow and scatter among them, buy (as every beginner in market analysis knows) markedly different bundles of goods at different stages; no one is in the market for a car every day; nor is a family in that for a coffin more than at odd intervals in a lifetime – these high platitudes drop with a thud on our theoretical, constant populations, with firmly settled preferences, and needing only information about relative prices in order to exercise their preferences.

We ought rather to assume that, at any one time, and, therefore, right through even our long-run analysis, some fair proportion of consumers of a good, will, typically, still be discovering their 'want' of it; and that they will in fact discover what their preferences are, and how they balance up against their available income, only in the market-place itself. This may be pressed even further. The inchoateness of demand is much more pervasive even than suggested by the transiency of the population to which I have referred. Any regard for the supposedly self-interested procedures of shopkeepers, or, in the case of 'purer' theorists, even the exercise of our ancient privilege of introspection, should convince us that, even though our general dispositions may be settled, we nevertheless leave a good deal open, respecting the choice of commodity which we actually buy now to satisfy our 'wants', which are often general rather than specific in character.

It follows that we should regard the demand for any particular commodity, broadly defined, and still more the demand for any brand of it, as often rather chancy if we look only at the functional relation with price. It is, then, not surprising that econometricians are also beginning to suggest that, if there are patterns of price/quantity behaviour in consuming units, they run in terms of groups of commodities, rather than in terms of individual commodities within the group.

The conclusion I draw from this is that our demand theory should not run in terms of consumers, as though they are in equilibrium with respect to all else but the price of the good we are especially considering, and then as moving decisively from equilibrium to equilibrium as the price of the good changes. We should allow, in our constructions, for the effect of market organisation and practices. The dispositions of consumers should be seen as steadied into the actual purchase of this or that, in aggregates which are relatively stable, just because of the activities and organisation of the retail market, and the opportunities for purchase actually held out to them as people move around. It will be seen that I argue that what we analyse as mere price changes may well affect this organisation of the market in which the goods are sold.

I illustrate the importance of non-price variables chiefly with reference to stocks (inventories), for this example will show the importance for demand theory of structural features of industry which are too frequently regarded as 'mere' matters of organisation and disregarded in systematic theory. Obviously, the mere presence of stocks affects the choices actually made with regard to the goods which, in our usual analyses, an industry stands ready to 'supply'. Accordingly, even simple theoretical models with only one demand function for a whole 'industry' should have a third dimension relating to stocks, alongside the price and quantity to which we normally confine ourselves. But, once we add this dimension, there will be a change in the quality and character of our theory. We may no longer discuss the trade in a commodity as a whole, with all demand prisoned between one set of co-ordinates. Still less may we argue loosely, as is done in many discussions of retail trade, in terms of whole classes of commodities as though they were but one good similarly analysed.

It is, I hope, a very obvious point, put that way – but recall how many books, even advanced and specialist texts, offer models with demand functions in which prices and quantities are the only variables! At the same time, a zeal for the practical application of these models may be shown in the partisan discussion of changes in retail trade, such as the advent of supermarkets. According to the very advantages our zealots ascribe to these, their advent will affect such relevant matters as the quantities and types of stocks, where these will be available to the buyer, and the kinds of shops which will carry them. How, then, can we discuss these matters as we do within the single demand curve for 'the' commodity in a simple model – should we not allow for overall demand being affected? In sum, the position and characteristics of the demand function at any outlet, and the position and characteristics of the aggregate demand for a good (having regard to price), will be determined by the total system of distribution and change with it.

We shall not rid ourselves of this shoddy sort of analysis until we learn to be suspicious of the conflation of industrial structure in which we so commonly indulge. I here therefore name *conflated models* as a prevalent source of error. The single models of retail trade which we have just discussed are an example of conflation at the retail stage. Even our confusion of buyers and consumers may be seen as an example of analytical conflation. Names *are* powerful things, but I believe that we economists have been easier prey to the black magic which the noun 'consumer' has for us just because we find it easy to slip into conflated models of industrial situations and, indeed, teach and argue in terms of them without the slightest hesitation.

The more general kind of conflated model is, indeed, where we discuss a whole 'industry' as an entity. Because this is so much a habit with us, I must emphasise that I really am criticising what we take without question – the ready way in which we bring together the whole price/output economics of a producing industry and of its wholesale and retail stages, within a single pair of co-ordinates. We should stop and think every time we allow the use of but two curves to analyse an industry – with one curve conflating, as it were, all the successive markets into one market, in terms of the demand generated by the final consumer; so that the other curve brings together all the stages of production and distribution down to the point where the product is on final sale.

Of course, our ready acceptance of this device goes back to the cradle of our methodology, which each generation reoccupies in its formative classes – the marginalist equilibrium analysis of a perfectly competitive, stationary state! There, it is legitimate technically to refer all other levels of demand to the consumers' demand in the final market; so that we may conflate on to the demand side, and let consolidated functions on the supply side react as though a homogeneous industry were all that is involved, with each single firm in the conflated model apparently deciding the whole chain of production and marketing operations.

It should be clear enough, once it is questioned, that such a conflation lacks formal validity in monopolistic competition analysis, and I shall not pause over this; the major points will emerge in a more general criticism of vertically conflated models of the kind we have been discussing. The chief point I wish to make is that it is vertical conflation which makes orthodox equilibrium analysis so innocent of industrial structure, whether as between businesses at the same level in the industry, or as between businesses at different levels in an industry complex. Like unscientific Peer Gynts, 'All beings are alike' to us.

I have already suggested that the conditioning of economists to unstructured conflated models explains why the question of business demand did not arise to throw doubts on the general validity of monopolistic competition kinds of analysis. I am sure that these conflated simplifications explain why, although so few economists have paid special theoretical attention to retail trade, any one of us, at the drop of a hat, is ready to make hasty deductions concerning it. I take as an example the treatment of manufacturers' brands as though such goods were on an exact par with the other goods, as we say, 'of the same kind' with which they compete in the shops. From this has followed an absence of theoretical appreciation of their competitive importance – indeed, of the character of competition at the retail level which they mark.

In the absence of manufacturers' brands, consumers would be served only by goods whose specifications were determined by the direct interests of retailers, and the competition of manufacturers could affect the final market only by subserving the interests of retailers. Technical monopolistic competition being put on one side, one still could not deny that in strict analysis each shop would have, in some sense, its 'own' brands; and one should recognise that the rewards to a shop from being 'different' might well conflict with those from being an efficient distributor. There must be some conflict between all considerations affecting retailers and those of the economy of standardisation beyond the scales of individual retail firms, which latter would affect only manufacturers directly.

In the presence of manufacturers' brands, the choices open to the consumer are extended by goods whose specifications are immediately influenced by production considerations. The consumer can affect the final balance, weighing up differences in qualities and prices, only so long as manufacturers' goods are sufficiently represented in the shops where he makes his choice. Because of our conflated models and our inadequate consideration of this structural aspect of competition, we have not asked ourselves what conditions might favour the competition from manufacturers' brands and we have indeed worked in terms of models where the advantage of such competition is presumed away.

In view of the almost universal cocksureness of our profession on this point, dare I refer to the question of Fair Trade – resale price maintenance? Have we not overlooked one aspect of the possible freedom of a manufacturer to restrict price competition on his brand? While your ire is perhaps roused, I add most firmly that this does not mean that the manufacturer is free necessarily to set an *un*competitive price for his goods in their retail market as a whole, as against other brands, whether of other manufacturers or of retail shops themselves. It is only our ready use of settled differentiated demand curves, which I am questioning, which makes it possibly appear feasible for him to do so. (Nor does it mean that I am saying that fair trade is always positively beneficial.)

To come back to relevant argument: all our accepted theory tends to cause us to assume that shops' own brands may differ in the eye of the consumer; and I do not see why I should not appeal to this prejudice of ours in order to stress an important matter which our analysis overlooks.

In so far as shops are offering manufacturers' brands, then, shops really are competing with identical goods. It follows that, in unrestricted competition, these goods offer special opportunities for price competition and — another way of looking at it — they will involve special risks of price competition. In this situation, different classes of shop will be in different positions with regard to manufacturers' brands as a class: those selling such goods as only a part of their range may well gain from price cutting, when they allow for extra trade in other goods, which such price cutting will promote. Shops which would otherwise concentrate more on manufacturers' brands would be especially vulnerable to such price competition.

If you feel a little restive with me, perhaps that is because one thinks naturally of this competition as a matter between shops; leave it there, and one tends to favour the usual *prima facie* argument — that consumers gain by any price cuts and that, if price cuts occur, the demand for the brands concerned will be greater, so that the manufacturer himself will gain in extra trade at his own wholesale prices, and only the shops which prove themselves less efficient in this competition will lose. This, familiar as it is, to English ears anyway, is indeed exactly what I meant earlier by bad *prima facie* argument. The shift in retail trade which this sort of argument accepts in its usual terms of 'less efficient' and 'more efficient' kinds of retailer, may not be neutral in its effects on other aspects of competition; may very well weaken the competition from manufacturers' brands by making it more difficult for manufacturers to sell even the same quantities of their goods. Those outside the small circle of leading brands, may well find it impossible. And the possibilities of new entry are to be seen as very adversely affected.

Given the inchoateness of much demand, which I stressed earlier in this chapter, we must allow that there may be goods whose demand will depend on the extent to which they are (a) widely stocked, and/or (b) offered by retailers carrying an assorted range of such goods. In these cases, free price competition, by reducing the numbers of outlets in general or the numbers of such specialist retailers, would reduce the total demand for a brand, and the influence of manufacturing conditions in competition at the retail level will diminish. How very self-evident these points seem when spelt out! The more confident, then, am I in my conclusion that it is no accident but a consequence of our orthodox methodology, that professional discussion of the effects of resale price maintenance on prices and competition at the retail level, shows no awareness at all of even the possibility that these circumstances can arise; or that mistaken conclusions need to be guarded against by detailed discussion in terms of individual kinds of goods likely to be the subject of this restrictive practice.

Much more could be said and by way of other examples, of how emaciated is the concept of competition which we refer to the ring fence of single, static demand curves, inside which we totally suppress the essential competitiveness of different kinds or levels of business. The paradox is that, with our professional veneration of competition, we cannot accommodate important forms of competition in practice except in models intended to exhibit, not competition, but monopoly. Nor can we exhibit even the effects of price competition, which we purport to analyse, within the structured arrangements of everyday life. (Indeed, look up structure in the average index, and there are mere references to number of firms presently competing.) Against this, I say that, in the real world, the structure of an industry is the essential framework within which to understand its competitiveness. Given freedom of entry, a topic which I have yet to discuss, it is indeed competitiveness which may produce the structure which our methodology compels us to ignore.

But before leaving conflated models in order to discuss entry conditions, there are two other matters I should touch on. One and an important one is the question of advertising. This activity is, of course, often closely associated with manufacturers' brands; our conflated models cause us to overlook in our analysis the possibility that advertising may promote the competitive influence of manufacturers' brands, in our concentration upon the creation of preferences which we analyse in terms of the mere diversion of demand as between goods which we treat as belonging to the same class. As we observed earlier, the demand curves in which we analyse such diversion of demands treat demand as otherwise a certain function of the price of each commodity alone. When we discussed the effects of the inchoateness and instability of ordinary demand, I refrained from pointing out how weak our attitude to advertising had to be; in orthodox simple models, we can analyse advertising only in terms of persuading the consumer to do *this*, when he would rather otherwise have done *that* – to buy Jones's Blanco Beer, when he would otherwise have bought Brown's Bronco Beer. A more realistic and more sophisticated view of demand would suggest that advertising and other selling activities may be necessary if individual sellers are to realise demand opportunities of that stability which our usual analysis takes for granted. We have already seen the economic function of stocks – advertising may be one of the factors facilitating the enforcement of necessary levels and locations of stocks. But this is additional to the effects of advertising even as between firms at the same level of analysis, in stabilising that short-period division of custom without which the firm may not be able to achieve that maximum economy of production which our cost curves assume. To this, we have to add the less obvious function which may be even more important – permitting the competition for the consumers' dollar in the final retail market stage to be more susceptible to the influence of production economies than it would otherwise be.

The second serious limitation on our economic analysis which our conflated models produce, I think, is our tendency to analyse the behaviour of an individual business in terms of the decisions of *the* 'entrepreneur' conceived as running it. Although this may seem natural enough in the abstract firms of our conflated models, it is not so defensible that we should carry over to the real world an obstinate inclination to translate everything of economic moment within a business in terms of the functions, as it were, of a single desk at one level. Quite apart from this view contributing, as I think it does, to the afflatus of what we call 'top' management, the myopia which accompanies it conduces towards our modern monopolistic simplification of business economics – and opens the door to a lot of what I regard as unanalytical nonsense besides.

In this connexion, I have appealed to phenomena which show what I have named 'internal competition' – competitiveness, as between managements and departments, which exists because it contributes to career drives as well as to that internal economy which our supply functions take for granted, and in a way which would not be possible as simple routine in business competing in a changing world; internal competition, moreover spills out in external aggressiveness. It will be clear enough that orthodox marginalist equilibrium methodology left enough scope for this point to be made by me as a novelty, obvious though it is once one has seen internal competition in action *and* realised the analytical function of what one is seeing. There are, equally, positive theoretical implications which I shall not now pursue.

Looking back over the errors which I have brought up against our orthodox methodology, the most common characteristic is a tendency to underplay the possible reach of actual competition. This general tendency has itself been reinforced by the handling of the question of new-entry competition, and, here again, our difficulties would appear to go back to the conceptual limitations of our basic models, starting with perfect competition analysis, where marginalist equilibrium requirements enforced rising marginal-cost and supply curves. From the earliest beginnings of the modern methodology then, new entrants, and potential new entrants, have been conceived of as being, smaller, more ignorant, less efficient, etc. than firms already established in an industry.

These prejudices passed over into monopolistic competition analysis and into such work as Fellner's, dealing with collusive oligopolies. We may note also that the particular demand curves, which are a fundamental concept since monopolistic competition came along, not only mark an assumed monopolistic protection of individual businesses against one another and against new entrants, but by the same token imply weaknesses in competitive power. In this way we have come to play down the forces of competition within an industry — stressing an analytical uniqueness of existing products and analysing away the power to duplicate which is conferred by the freedom to differentiate.

It is very important for the understanding of the history of economic thought that the classical monopoly and the classical and monopolistic competition oligopoly models allow of no competition from the outside at all. The classical kind of box of oligopoly toys works, in so far as it works at all, only on the basis of that unreal exclusion. The modern developments of the theory of games are stigmatised by the same defects, and a lot of steam goes out of that literature once one starts discussing new-entry conditions.

Once, however, we allow as a general matter any doubts about the long-run strength of barriers arising from buyers' preferences, as we must certainly do in the case of business demand, and as I think observable processes suggest we should do in the case of consumer demand, the barriers to competition from within and without industries topple — and they must be weaker, within an industry, anyway, if we allow any serious force to oligopolistic relationships. I have therefore been obliged to call attention to the potential power of *cross-entry competition*, as I call it, within an industry. But this is only one neglected aspect of the *potential competition* which may face any business, despite its established goodwill, and, indeed, must set limits to the protection we ascribe to the latter.

It is significant of the strength of our conceived prejudices that the work of Bain is vitiated by his concentration upon completely new enterprises and his neglect of competitive enterprise from businesses, already established elsewhere, which competition may have especially high potential strength because such businesses may draw for new ventures on facilities already created in their parent businesses, and even borrow goodwill from these. It is consistent with this defect that Bain also, as Elizabeth Brunner has pointed out,[1] refuses to treat as competitive with an established industry the creation of supply facilities in its customer businesses. All this has been in issue since 1949 at least, when I raised it, and it is perhaps a melancholy tribute to the strength of our methodology that these issues have not been followed with any close interest among our profession. Entry conditions must be one of the major areas to be 'revisited' if we are to assess our methodology with any fresh outlook.

CONCLUSIONS
In conclusion, I shall refer in rather warmer terms to the state of our science as I interpret it. I am glad that I was brought up in an earlier age when economics was taught as an exciting subject with problems which were worthy of continuous study, and against a background of teaching of the history of economic thought so that one understood or tried to understand the linkages between the questions which arose in any age and the methods of analysis adopted by its economists. I regret the orthodoxy which I have been attacking, not only because of the errors which I have been describing but also for its hierarchical arrogance. I am first of all a theorist and yield to no one in my assessment of the importance of theory and conceptual work. I regret some current tendency on the part of some of our most distinguished teachers, not merely to raise theory in the abstract, above theorizing with an eye on the real world, but also to encourage young theorists to devote themselves to the mere elaboration of the structure of theory established within our recent methodology. I have often heard both tendencies justified with reference to the role of pure theory in natural science, which I believe to be absurdly *un*-justified.

It may be that our pretensions to being a more mature science may be justified *vis-à-vis* some of our struggling sister social sciences, though one could wish for less arrogance in the claim. It is certainly not the case that *our* pure theory can be profitably defended with natural-scientific analogies. For historical reasons, economic methodology has so far developed quite the other way round from that of natural science. In natural science, broadly speaking, the earlist theory has been most concerned with matters of local detail, corresponding to our micro-level subjects. (The simple law of gravitation applies to the falling apple which it is said inspired it.) In due time, and after much work concerned with natural phenomena, earlier scientific generalisations have been superseded by generalisations of successively wider scope, progressively extending, as it were, the pure theory on which applied workers in the more detailed areas can draw. But the older generalisations are not, in the ordinary sense, falsified. The analysis of gravitation now involves the complex behaviour of the whole cosmos, yet modern scientists will not fall into noticeable error if they discuss falling apples as falling apples.

Economics started the other way round, with a concern for the macro-level problems which bothered both statesmen and the enlightened-citizen amateurs who were our earliest, and among our greatest, economists. The achievements of the perfect competition analysis which gave formal shape to classical theory have been remarkable at this so-general level of abstraction, and it should be noted that the work of Keynes, ignoring the imperfect competition revolution, proceeded within the same system. It is here that our methodology, as I have noted, gave us what is *the* characteristic professional vision of the economist; and looking back on the practical wisdom of such economists as Henry Clay, I doubt if the sophistications of modern training have been more fruitful when *our* pupils go out into the real world. What concerns me now, however, is that our modern micro-level theory has tended to fracture that vision.

But is it small wonder that we should go into error, when we apply a macro-level methodology to micro-level problems? What has led to good working approximations at one level may be expected to mislead in a more detailed application, and this chapter has provided sufficient examples of how we are misled.

I suggest that, because we are so concerned nowadays with micro-level problems, we should start the other way round and try to build theory expressly for the micro-level of the firm and the industry. At the end of the day, we shall, I suggest, do more — we shall find our way in a scientific fashion to new macro-level theory which will embrace and be consistent with our lower-level generalisations, in the way that more advanced natural-science generalisations usually are consistent with theirs. Then indeed we may find more scope for that division between pure and applied work after which, at the moment, I believe we do wrong to hanker.

# 2 Competitive Prices, Normal Costs and Industrial Stability*

This chapter presents a simplified model of normal-cost price theory. It will be concerned with the positive theory of the firm and the competitive industry which Andrews developed first in 1949, in consequence of our empirical studies, as an alternative to the static marginalist micro-equilibrium theory of the firm.[1] There is, clearly, an investment theory parallel to the price theory, and we have published an outline of such a theory.[2] More recently, the same system of thinking has been applied in retail trade theory.[3] But today, as I have indicated, I shall not look beyond the theory of manufacturers' prices, seen as determined by long-run factors (or, at all events, non-short-run factors). It is a *general* model, and is only presented in outline here, but I hope it will show some of the interesting things which we think we can handle.

## THE MODEL

From the point of view of method in the abstract, the model must, of course, stand within the critique of orthodox theory which Andrews developed in Chapter 1; that is, the individual firm will not be analysed as in a state of full equilibrium, whether marginalist or otherwise. But this disequilibrium of the firm must be consistent with industrial stability. To explain this, we must also explain what conditions will lead to industrial *in*stability, and I shall therefore touch on relevant aspects of the theory of the structure of an industry.

I suggest that other, more detailed criteria to be satisfied by the model may be derived from the history of thought in the industrial pricing area. First, it should embody those characteristics which made pure-competition theory of practical significance, and which were also present in the simple model of Chamberlin's monopolistic competition in the large group, and which made the latter seem at first an acceptable substitute for pure-competition theory as a general model.

This means that the model should feature: relatively stable short period prices; and prices which are 'cost compatible' — this is a shorthand phrase

*Given as a paper to a seminar at Harvard University, March 1966.

to cover the phenomena which Andrews has summarized (I quote from *On Competition in Economic Theory*, p. 17). Prices should be 'compatible with one another, in the sense that commodities with similar specifications [are] ... sold at much the same prices, and also that prices of commodities with different specifications [can] ... be analysed as compatible with each other on a cost basis.' (I note that the non-simple model of Chamberlin's large group, when there are unequal preferences, would not satisfy this last condition.)

Second, the model must include those special characteristics which made the Chamberlin general model realistically preferable to the classical pure-competition model: it must permit decreasing costs to the firm as compatible with industrial stability; and it must recognise the differentiation of products with buyers' preferences.

Third, we must cover those further characteristics of *actual* industrial competition which have been recognised in post-Chamberlinian discussion:

(i) The model should treat oligopoly as the normal situation.

(ii) It should be consistent with practical pricing procedures, as reported for example, by Hall and Hitch in consequence of the work of the old Oxford Economists' Research Group. (Because of the persistent misunderstanding of those procedures as 'full cost', I quote a summary of these findings by Andrews, secretary of the Research Group then: 'Business men generally settled their prices by procedures which were based on their average costs, determining in various ways a pricing margin to be added to their current average prime costs.' (*On Competition in Economic Theory*, p. 33).

(iii) At the prices thus established, firms are to offer an elastic supply of their products.

Other characteristics consistent with empirical work are:

(iv) Firms are characteristically multi-product, even within fairly narrow classes of goods.

(v) The demand functions for industry groups of commodities are relatively inelastic. It also follows from this and (i) above that the analysis, although long-run in basis, has

(vi) to be consistent with kinked short-run demand functions for individual firms.

Since I have deliberately analysed the characteristics of our model on a historico-methodological basis, it may be convenient, even at the cost of some repetition, if I summarise the leading characteristics afresh. They are:

(i) Long-run decreasing costs to the firm.
(ii) Practical pricing procedures in which prices are calculated with reference to average costs in some way or other.
(iii) Prices which are compatible with each other on a normal-cost basis.
(iv) Elastic supply from the firm at those prices.
(v) Differentiation of products, with buyers' preferences.
(vi) Firms which are multi-product, even when producing only narrow classes of goods.
(vii) Markets which are characterised by relatively inelastic commodity demand curves; and by oligopolistic relations between businesses; and yet also by short-term stability of prices.

The model which I shall actually present will run formally in terms of a narrowly specified commodity, corresponding to the basis on which individual prices are, in fact, quoted by producers. The cost functions must, therefore, be formally in terms of a commodity of the same narrowness of specification. I note that what I shall later say in terms of the normal-cost/price compatibility of diverse commodities issuing from the same basic production processes will mean that we need not regard this as an unduly restrictive limitation on the scope of the cost curve. In practice, one can move fairly freely from analysis of individual costings to consideration of the broad process costs which characterise firms, and so to available cost statistics.

I have said that the model is concerned with manufacturers' prices — strictly only in the market at point of manufacture. This is consistent with orthodox models, so may simply be accepted by most economists; but Andrews has criticised such models for their conflation of the retail and manufacturing stages and indicated the kind of errors which result from this. In realistic terms, such a model of manufacturers' prices covers producers' goods and unbranded consumers' goods sold to other businesses. The difficulty with branded consumers' goods is that forms of competition among retailers may affect the demand conditions at point of manufacture. Any retailer is selling a variety of goods, and the customer in any shop is exposed to the purchase of more than one good at a time, so that the calculation of each must run in terms of the overall shopping opportunity or 'basket of goods'. Thus, for example, the demand for the branded good of a manufacturer may be affected by the retailer cutting the price of that brand, as a loss leader, for the sake of the effect on the sale of other goods in the shop. But I do not here wish to get involved in the theory of demand for a commodity at the retail level. Our model can cover branded consumers' goods if we make the assumption that here, too, final retail prices are close functions of prices at point of manufacture, so that the branded goods of one manufacturer can be kept in simple competition, at their respective prices, with all other brands.

## DEMAND

On the demand side, we assume that manufacturers look to their long-run demand, and we assume that buyers in the long run are rational.

I would justify these assumptions, in summary, on the following basis. First, a manufacturing firm is not normally interested in the very short-run view; it will have a considerable stake in manufacturing assets, essentially long term in character, so that pricing and investment decisions will be taken with a view to their long-term effects. Nor can it be argued that maximising profits in each of a series of short runs will be the best way to maximise long-run profits, for the long-run position is not ind^pendent of what is done in the short run; for example, a high price in one period may seem profitable then, but may lead to a smaller future market. Maximising the immediate advantage may be appropriate to the peddler of temporary novelties. Such people do not need the goodwill of continuing custom, but businesses offering regular product lines to a regular clientele do need it.

In the loose way in which the idea of 'long-run' demand curves has been formulated, it will generally be agreed, I think, that the long-run demand for the product of an individual business must be more elastic than the short-run demand (for, in the long run, any substitutes will compete more effectively, and buyers will be better informed about them). The normal construction of a falling demand curve for the individual firm can apply only where there are irrational buyers' preferences. I define rationality as the condition that a commodity will not *in the long run* continue to be purchased from one source, if another source will offer an identical commodity, in terms of specifications, at a lower price. In the long run, for a general model, it seems a much more reasonable working assumption that customers are generally rational than that they are generally irrational.

This for the following reasons. First, a high proportion of sales are of producers' goods or intermediate goods which go to businesses for their own use. We must assume these customers to be as rational as buyers as we assume them to be as suppliers. Second, the bulk of all consumers' goods are sold through the medium of another business, and not direct from manufacturer to final consumer. These intermediate businessmen are experts in their own line and will see that they get value for money, both for their own profit and to secure goodwill for their establishment from their own customers.

Even the final consumer may not be taken as likely to persist in irrational behaviour in the long run. The most difficult case, undoubtedly, is the case of branded consumers' goods, presented to the consumer with all the resources of persuasive advertising. But a lot of consumers' goods are bought regularly in small quantities and are relatively cheap; while advertising may induce people to *try* a particular brand, they will not continue to buy it, unless they are satisfied with its real quantities when tried. It is, moreover, with respect to this class of goods that one needs most to bear in mind the fluidity of consumer demand as a regular feature of the market.

Where a mistake is likely to be more costly and has to be lived with – the case of consumers' durable capital goods – is just where consumers do take trouble to survey the alternatives, take advice from a number of shops or other consumers, read a consumers' guide before purchase, etc. There is a relatively narrow range of consumers' commodities where advice or knowledge-in-use is weak against persuasive advertising, but surely we cannot build a whole theory of demand on commodities like cosmetics and patent medicines.

I would argue that the majority of consumers are rational for most of their purchases most of the time. However, we do not even have to assume that a majority of consumers are rational; if even 10 per cent behave rationally, there will be a big increase in demand waiting for any individual seller who assumes rationality rather than irrationality, and so it is unlikely to be profitable to assume the latter.

The recognition of goodwill does not contradict the assumption of rationality. We indeed assume that all commodities are differentiated, and that buyers will have preferences for the products of particular producers. Other things being equal, a buyer will prefer to deal with the same suppliers; there are advantages in personal contacts and in familiarity of dealings. But this is *given the price*, not without regard to price. We cannot assume that a buyer will persist in buying a good, long run, even if its price is higher than could be obtained elsewhere. Goodwill does not necessarily give the power to raise prices, but it divides the market between suppliers at a given level of prices. Incidentally, this was also Marshall's view of goodwill.

The conclusion is, therefore, that, long run, no buyer will pay more for the commodity than the price at which another supplier would offer a commodity with identical specifications. This means that we assume that the industry is easy to enter so far as barriers on the demand side are concerned.

CONDITIONS OF SUPPLY

Turning to the supply side of the market: here also barriers to entry are normally low, far lower than it is customary to regard them as being. We have too narrow a concept of entry. New entry may come not only from new firms, which it is too easy to see as small and weak and thus uninfluential, but from existing firms in other industries who are looking for further profitable outlets, or are anxious for diversification for its own sake (and in these cases barriers from economies of scale and from finance will be relatively unimportant). Such entry competition also comes from what Andrews has called cross-entry, from firms in the same industry, breaking across sub-markets.

With this wider concept of entry, the time scale for actual entry for a newcomer who has existing production facilities, access to markets, know-how and finance, will be relatively short. When we say that, in the long run, a firm has to be competitive or go out, remember that this is not the long run 'when we are all dead'. In industrial competition, the long-run situation which it will have to face should be near enough to quicken a threatened firm into action.

Nor is it necessary, of course, for there to be *actual* new entry for an industry to be competitive; indeed, actual entry would be a sign of some disequilibrium, either of supply or of price. We assume that other potential suppliers of this commodity would construct or convert facilities to its production, so long as they could do as well with it as with other products.

Thus, it is not even necessary to assume consumer rationality (as I do because I think it realistic) to get the same analytical result. In the case of free-entry and cross-entry, the weighing up of prices against objective differences of goods is done by producers in competition with each other, who will move into the markets which are more profitable. In these circumstances, only producers and not consumers are required to be rational.

We interpret the consequence of our assumptions as entailing a definite long-run limit to price, as in Figure 1. The level of this line, which is not a demand curve, will be the price at which any other supplier would offer an identical commodity to the present customers or, which is the same thing, the entry-forestalling price at which new entry will just not take place. If a firm puts its price too high, others can underquote it, and in time it will get continuously falling sales. This is an unstable situation, which I shall comment on later.

Equally, it will not normally pay the firm to put its price any lower. Since goodwill operates at the competitive price level, if it puts its price to

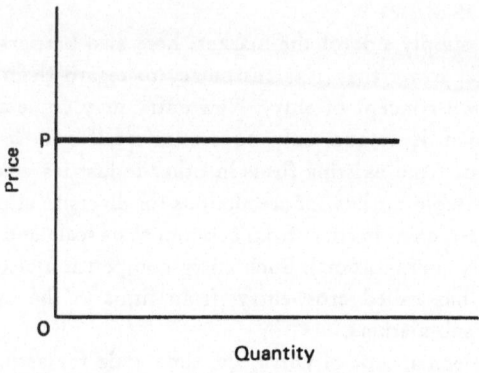

*Figure 1*

this level, its market will not be reduced by losses to others. We assume, it will be remembered, conditions of oligopoly and a relatively inelastic overall demand function for the group of competitors. Thus, if the one firm cuts price below the given level, its rivals will follow and cut price too, so that each will get only its share of the inelastic general market. The market for each firm is therefore limited at the given level of price, and may be treated as constant, at any time, actual or in prospect. (See Figure 2, where there is a line cutting off the market of the firm in its commodity.)

Suppose that the producer, not being able to know the entry-forestalling limit of price with precision, puts his price at a lower level, and let us assume that it is not just a mistake which he will seek to correct. Perhaps, he is deliberately intending to be on the safe side, in view of the serious

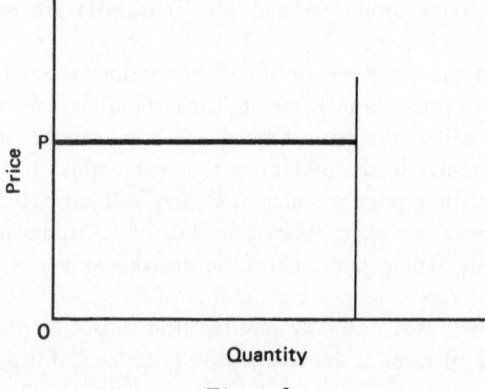

*Figure 2*

consequences of making a mistake the other way, and he is satisfied with less return than others. First, in an oligopoly situation, others will be forced to follow him down. Second, he is at the same time adopting a lower standard of what is a necessary margin of profit to attract him to the production of *other* firms' products; that is, the price level at which he would enter their markets is lowered. But each oligopolistic sub-market is linked to others, and a few firms adopting a low-price policy will determine standards for the whole chain of markets which make up the industry. Thus their price becomes the new maximum price level.

The firm stands ready to supply all it can at this price. Its market is limited by existing goodwill, but it will normally be pushing at the limit. To explain why a business will be willing to produce whatever the market will take, we have to turn to generalisations about the behaviour of costs.

## COSTS

The generalisations about behaviour of costs are based on our own empirical experience, and there is considerable other evidence now in support. We see the long-run cost curve as falling continuously throughout its length as scale increases, sharply to begin with for small scale-sizes, and then less and less steeply, as in Figure 3. The precise slopes will vary according to the product and the industry, but very small sizes of plant will have substantially higher costs than plants which are relatively not so much bigger. This reflects the influence of technical economies of scale; once the major economies of flow production are available to the firm, further major mechanisation can only be applied to ancillary processes, such as handling and transport; and while, at any point, some further technical economies are likely always to be open to the firm, they will

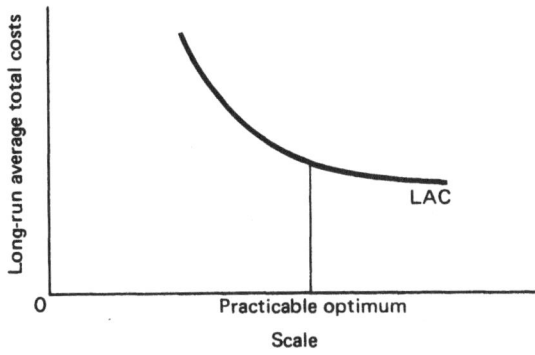

*Figure 3*

become relatively less important, and may be attainable only in very large discontinuous steps.

Those who assert a U-shaped long-run cost curve appeal to management diseconomies with increasing scale, which are seen as counterbalancing any technical economies. But, surely, it is wrong to think of management as a fixed quantity which can, therefore, be over-extended, long run. There are different techniques and systems of management, and, as long as a system appropriate to size of firm is employed, there is no reason why it should be less efficient – and certainly not progressively less and less efficient with increasing scale.

Further, even if it were true that management diseconomies increase with scale, these would not ordinarily come into a business's *ex ante* calculation of its long-run cost position on expansion. No management is going to assume that it cannot manage a bigger business so well, provided that it is given more staff and time to adjust, so that for forward planning and decision-making, it is the influence of the technical cost curve which is most important.

There will be some point of scale which represents a 'practicable optimum' position; beyond this point the rate of fall of the average cost curve will be considerably more gentle, and a substantial increase in scale of output thereafter would be necessary to achieve significant reductions in cost. In an established industry, firms may be assumed to be of at least practicable optimum size. If they are of less than this size, there are conditions of instability and we shall discuss this later. At present, we assume stability, and therefore that firms will be operating at or beyond practicable optimum scale. The conclusion we need, to establish which will give elastic supply from the firm at a given price, is simply that in the long run the firm would think it could always make more profit by producing more at any given price.

At the same time, however, the fall in the long-run cost curve beyond the practicable optimum point is gentle for any increase in scale which is achievable by an individual firm's own actions. There is the further point which realistic analysis must remember, that even with good estimates of what costs will be at some significantly larger scale, the firm will, of course, require time to learn fully to exploit the possibilities at that scale. It is therefore reasonable for a firm to price as though its long-run average costs would be constant, although hoping to do somewhat better than that if it actually grows. These considerations explain why businesses should settle their prices for existing products, as practical inquiry finds they do, in terms of their current short-run costs.

The behaviour of short-run costs is therefore of explicit importance.

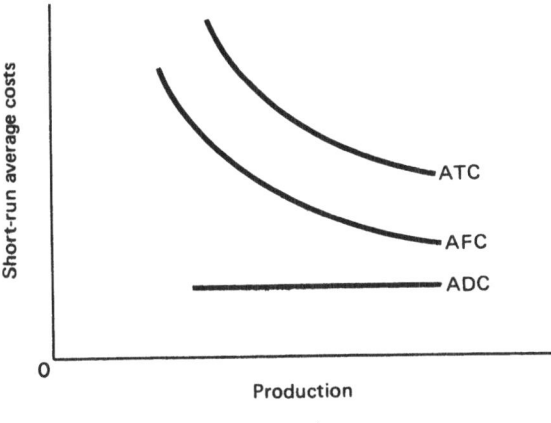

*Figure 4*

Empirical work has shown that businesses assume that average direct costs per unit, as 'costed' for any specific product, will be constant at any given time. This is explicable, if we reject the traditional concept of firms being organised to produce a certain 'point' of output at least cost, and when we recognise that firms will plan to have enough flexibility to produce economically a *range* of output.

In any production planning period, e.g. a year, a business must allow for fluctuations in output which may be large. Seasonal and secular conditions change. The business will wish to produce the range of output smoothly and to keep some reserve in hand to allow for breakdowns and repair of machinery. Further, it will wish to meet its market rather than lose goodwill and risk competitors getting established, if there is a surge of demand in its favour. The rising branch of the traditional U-shaped cost curve is therefore irrelevant to our model and, for pricing purposes, we may represent short-run costs, over the appropriate range, as in Figure 4: average direct costs constant per unit; overhead costs decreasing per unit, and, therefore, average total costs per unit decreasing.

At the upper end of the normal range of output, of course, in practice actual direct costs may start creeping upwards. An obvious example is the effect of overtime payments to labour. But these will not enter into price calculations, and therefore must not enter into our cost curves for price/output theory purposes; though such additions to costs will be relevant to income theory. For pricing theory, such additional costs as overtime payments, which are, of course, also excluded by the strict definitions of orthodox cost curves, come into the category of 'extra-ordinary costs' — costs which reflect circumstances or policies peculiar to

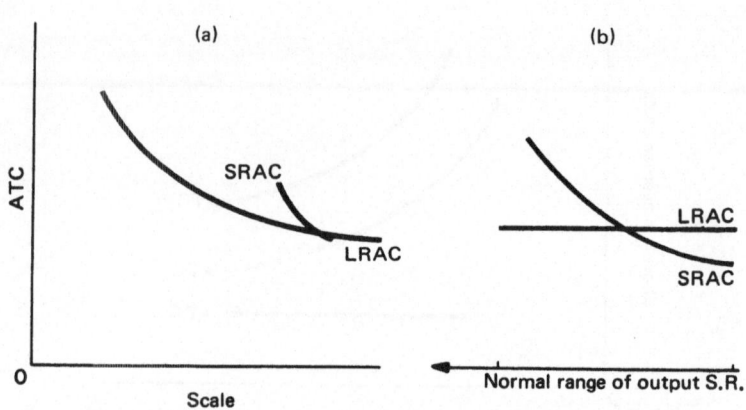

*Figure 5: (b) is a magnification of part of (a)*

the individual firm, which may not affect competitors, and hence are irrelevant to competitive pricing.

One consequence of this flexibility of short-run organisation is that the long-run cost curve is not the envelope of the short-run cost curves, as it is on the definitions of orthodox theory. In the short run, since plants will be organised to produce a normally fluctuating range of output rather than a precise point, the short-run cost curve will coincide with the long-run cost curve only at some point which we may loosely think of as the central point of the normal range. In the short run, if there is high demand, the market will be met at lower costs than would be feasible if the business were to plan to sustain such higher outputs for long periods. The short-run cost curve therefore cuts the long-run cost curve, the right-hand segment of the short-run curve lying below the long-run curve (Figures 5a and b).

It is of course the case that the level of the long-run cost curve in this model is higher than the long-run cost curve of orthodox theory; the investment in more flexible equipment and in reserve capacity has to be reflected in higher costs. But this is to compare costs for given points of output in given conditions. In actual situations, in the fluctuating real world, a plant which is organised for such a world will not depart so far from its theoretical cost curve as will the theoretical least-cost plant of orthodox theory.

Note that the business in the model is not in marginalist equilibrium; short-run marginal costs are constant, long-run marginal costs are falling, and demand is presented to the firm at a constant price.

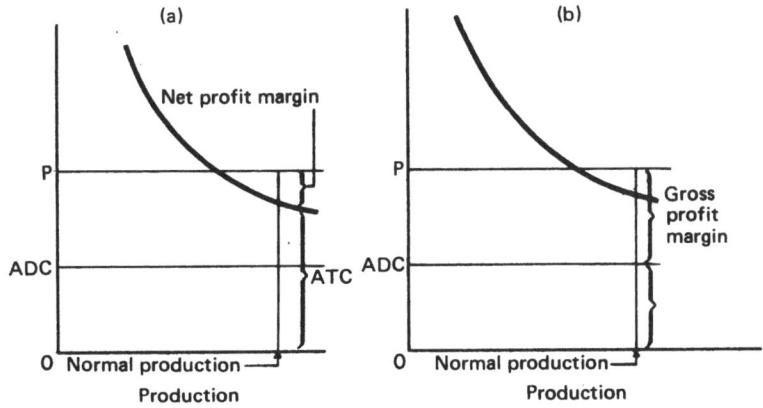

*Figure 6*

## PRICING

It will now be apparent that this model explains the sort of pricing practices which have been reported, all of which show businessmen settling their prices by procedures based on their average costs. There are various procedures, but they can be seen as falling into two broad types. In one type, a net profit margin is added to estimated average total cost at normal output (Figure 6a); in the other, to estimated average direct costs is added a gross profit margin to cover overheads and net profit (Figure 6b).

Other cost/price estimating procedures are found that reflect special circumstances; for instance, within type 6b, if the complexity of a business's work is associated with the labour side, it may take out separately estimates of materials costs and labour cost and allow for overhead costs a percentage based on the labour cost.

The approach to the price/costing procedure in 6b is more useful analytically, because it is assumed in the model that average direct costs, strictly defined, will be constant over the range of output for which the overhead facilities of the firm have been set up. Theorizing in terms of direct costs and the gross profit margin yielded at a given price enables one to avoid difficulties in realistic work which arise by reason of what Andrews has called the 'plasticity' of actual overhead costs. It is this, of course, which makes nonsense of the too simple idea of 'full costs' and the covering thereof. A firm will be able to estimate its level of average direct costs with fair precision, but the size of the gross profit margin to be added to this is a matter of much less exact calculation; overhead cost estimates have to be related to normal output in some way; and the gross profit margin, in whatever way it may be calculated, will be determined by the necessity to hit the right level of price for the market.

This is the basic model. It has been in terms of a single product, and the cost curves, of course, have been formally in terms of the firm making only the one product. Even for realistic work, we have to start in terms of the prices of individual products and the circumstances bearing upon them. In practice, of course, firms are multi-product. The one-product, basic theory of costs, however, does help us to understand the theoretical importance of standard costing procedures inside a multi-product firm: with constant average direct costs, and with overhead costs allocated on some common principle, so that relevant opportunity costs are represented, a multi-product firm has a way of calculating the current costs of any one product and comparing that with price. If it sees that another product, which it has the facilities to make, would yield it a reasonable profit, it will start moving into that product. Equally, other firms will have facilities so that they could make this firm's product and will move in if it will pay them to do so. Thus it is competition, and potential competition, in an industry which holds down the upper limit of price.

In terms of its effectiveness in competition, an industry must be defined more widely than those making identical products, and more widely even than businesses making products of the same class. In our terminology, it embraces all firms operating the same processes. Moreover, if one is to include all potential, as well as actual, competition, one needs to include firms with the know-how and experience to produce the same products, even if they have not at present the manufacturing processes; and this means that we must include customers as potential competitors, by virtue of potential vertical extension of their activities to replace suppliers or to compete with them.

Thus, the price of any product must not offer a prospective reward great enough to induce cross-entry from other existing producers, nor tempt vertical integration backwards or forwards, by a customer or supplier, let alone encourage entirely new enterprises to come in. These things may happen, but they are signs of disequilibrium.

If there is common technical equipment and experience, so that any firm *could* produce any one of a range of products, and if there is an awareness of the prices at which sales are being made, so that any firm can estimate the profitability of producing one product rather than another, the relationship between the prices for the range of products will have to be justified by differences in normal average costs of production, and we get the idea of normal profit for any commodity produced in that industry; normal profit being measured strictly from the viewpoints of individual firms.

In this way the complex of commodities from any one industry may be reduced to a cost-equivalent standard commodity, in the cost terms appropriate to any individual producer, and this is a realistic justification for using a single-product model as a reasonable abstraction.

## MARKET EQUILIBRIUM

The model thus leads to the idea of an equilibrium of price, and not of individual outputs. In the early days of an industry, there will be no such equilibrium, for all firms will be too small, and the situation will be unstable; anyone by cutting price, if he becomes aware of technological opportunity, could get considerable cost economies and an increased share of a rapidly expanding market. A market which grows too rapidly itself tends to increase the likelihood of instability, by making it easy for businesses temporarily to establish themselves, even though they are too small for long-run competition. To realise both the economies of larger-scale production and the entirely new strata of customers available for sufficiently drastic falls in prices of such new kinds of product, there is likely to be a period of warfare, after which the industries settle down to stable conditions with fewer firms at lower costs and prices.

In an established industry, where most firms will be at least of practicable optimum size, the too-small firm, or the 'inefficient' firm – the firm which, for whatever reason, has costs higher than the average – will not be able to get a price which will yield it normal net profits, and may not even cover all its costs. Its higher costs are 'extraordinary costs' which it will have to meet itself. (Strictly, *its* normal profit may thus be negative.) Equally, the relatively low-cost, 'efficient', firms will be anxious to grow by acquiring others' customers, by direct price competition or by inducements which we may analyse as equivalent to price cuts. The incentive to strengthen their hold on the market comes partly from hope of lower costs in the end; partly from fear that if they do not exploit a position some other competitor will; and partly from the push of internal competition – their own young men fighting for recognition and in the process, forcing growth on the business rather than opting for a quiet life.

The condition of stability is that a firm with lower costs shall not be able to drive out a higher-cost rival by offering a lower price. First, we must make the *caveat*, that actual businesses will achieve their ideal costs only to imperfect degrees, so that a particular smaller firm, for instance, may have lower costs than a particular larger one. This being said, however, sticking first to the ideal-cost situation, we have therefore to look at the structure of costs within the individual firm. If a lower-cost firm (which we will identify as the larger firm) becomes aggressive and cuts price, we must assume that the higher-cost firm (which we will identify as the smaller firm) follows suit, rather than lose market position; both then would have lower profits and may make losses. The question is, on the one hand, how low can price go before the larger firm cannot tolerate the effect on its profits, and, on the other hand, how low must price go in order to drive out the smaller firm?

The answer of simple orthodox theory is that firms can survive in the short run with losses up the extent of overhead costs, as long as price does not uncover average variable costs. But we have to look again at overhead costs. Too often, under the influence of simple models, overhead costs are discussed as though they were capital costs, *tout simplement*, whereas a high proportion are 'paying-out', or cash, costs. This is so for all staff salaries, of course, but, also, our usual generalisations do not recognise what a high proportion of labour is in fact overhead, and especially in modern industry. For example, in chemical processes, a reduction in throughput, unless it is so big that a whole section may be closed, will often make no difference to what we normally classify as process labour.

The more important capital, non-paying-out, costs are, the lower price would have to go to drive out the higher-cost firm. So we can expect a greater dispersion of sizes in industries whose technology is heavily dependent on capital facilities. Or, put the other way round, the more important *paying-out* overhead costs are, the less the disparity of size which will be compatible with the stability of an industry. The smaller firm may be at an additional disadvantage for survival, if economies of scale take the form of substitution of capital for other factors at an increasing rate; then smaller firms will have correspondingly higher proportions of paying-out costs, and a fall in price will make it relatively more difficult for them to survive.

The circumstances of each industry will differ, but there will be some practicable optimum scale for each, below which a firm would not be able to survive the competition from larger firms in its industry, which will be only too glad to divide its goodwill between them. Thus, in Figure 7, a firm of the scale of A is covering all its costs at $P_1$; it can survive if price falls to $P_2$, but not below that. At price $P_2$, firm B, on the other hand, is covering all its costs and could survive down to $P_3$, at which price only a giant firm, perhaps double B in size, could drive it out.

In this last discussion we have come closer to reality, but we are still, of course, in a world of abstract models. This is not the structure of an actual

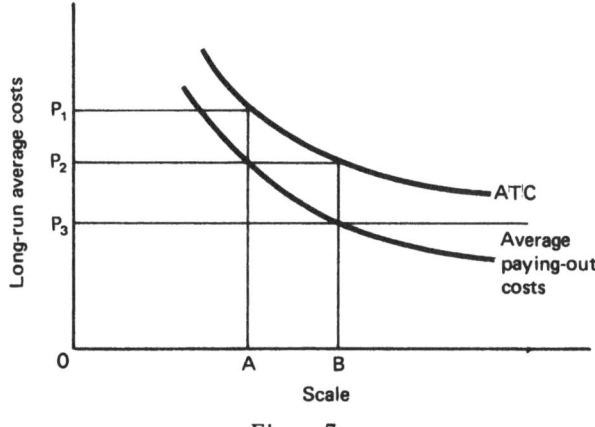

*Figure 7*

industry making goods of such and such a kind, but a guide from which we can start our analysis of any actual structure. There is much more that could be said about the actual survival of actual businesses with actual disparities of costs in the real world we have to work with. It is not possible to go into this in any detail now, but the question 'How is it that small firms survive?' was the question put to us in 1944 that started off twenty years' work.

So I may perhaps end with a few realistic notes. Very briefly, one important factor in the survival of small firms is the element of specialisation, disguised in our single-product analysis. The small firm can specialise on a product or a section of a market, whereas a large firm may have to serve the whole market. Thus, the small firm may get lower costs through a formal reduction of quality and in fact produce a product which is satisfactory for its own special market, which will never have occasion to discover other, irrelevant, qualities. For example, the smallest rayon firm in England specialised on the hosiery market; it could give its yarn the elasticity required for this market, but it never had to provide the tensile strength necessary for yarn being woven on a loom.

But the large firm has to produce for everybody the quality needed for its most exacting market; it is axiomatic that one cannot have more than one quality of work in one factory, and the large firm dare not risk lower-standard work spilling over into a market for which it was not intended.

Another way in which the small firm may get a higher gross margin is by specialising on the sections of the market which big firms, geared to long runs, and slower to turn round, will find it more costly to provide – repairs, jobs requiring special fitting to the individual customer, rush jobs, etc.

The large firm will find it a matter of prestige to be a technical leader, and to keep up to date technically, even at the expense of wasteful obsolescence. It will have to put money into research. The small firm is less likely to worry about keeping ahead technically, and may rely on getting the results of the big firm's research without doing its own. Moreover, the major economies of scale go with size of plant, and there will be much less disparity between sizes of plant than between sizes of firm. The large firm cannot extend a plant indefinitely in one area, because of pressures on the labour supply for one thing, and so is inevitably multi-plant. This may bring management complications and pressures from trade unions, to which smaller firms are less subject.

## SUMMARY

In the preceding paragraphs I have clearly been thinking of actual examples, and, if I had been thinking of others, I should have had to qualify what I have said by reference to other factors which would there have been relevant. This has, in any case, been taking us outside our strict terms of reference.

But I hope I have said enough to show how we must extend our model when we are dealing with a real firm or industry. In a real situation, we have to know in detail the structure of a firm's costs, its channels of distribution, the size structure of firms in the industry, and so on. But a model can suggest what questions to ask, and it must be consistent with reality.

To come back to our agenda, I have tried to outline a model which shows decreasing costs to the individual firm, firms not in marginalist equilibrium, differentiation of products – but no use of short-run demand curves; and, at the same time, rational cost-plus pricing. It is a model of competition, but it is not within the strait jacket of perfect competition, where we have to assume an infinitely large number of firms, all producing an identical product. The problem of oligopoly, which has occupied so much time of theorists since it was recognised as the situation most prevalent in the real world, disappears as an irrelevant technical problem, when one looks at the actual circumstances of competition, which is pervaded by oligopolistic relations between businesses, and open to the no-less pervasive threat of new entry. (It existed as a problem only because of the ruling out of new-entry competition.)

We think we now have a model of competition which applies to the relationships found in the real world.

# 3 Industrial Analysis Revisited

## INTRODUCTION

In the development of modern economic thought, industrial analysis appears to have been abandoned as a field for economic theory. Empirical studies of industries continue to be made but there is no theoretical attention to the industry level of analysis. It was always considered inadmissible, of course, by the theorist trained in the tradition of general equilibrium analysis, where the price of anything depends on the price and quantity produced of everything else, and every commodity is in competition with every other commodity for the consumer's dollar. The general equilibrium approach, true in itself, is not helpful when we wish to use theory to study the supply of commodities. There used to be a tradition of partial equilibrium analysis, handling the industry, which went back to Marshall. Marshall ostensibly handled 'competitive' industry, and he appears to have included in that category everything except statutory monopolies; but he did not develop a complementary theory of the firm, falling back on the construct of the representative firm when necessary. Later theorists pushed the logic of Marshallian competition to 'perfect competition' and thence to the equilibrium of the individual firm as well as of the industry; but in the process, of course, the 'industry' became emasculated to a rigid and restrictive definition of a large number of sellers all selling a homogeneous product. Chamberlin tried to preserve the concept of the industry or 'large group' even when recognising that products were differentiated, but he gave in to the attack of Triffin,[1] a general equilibrium theorist, and in his 'revisited' article wished to withdraw the emphasis on the large group and moved more towards the idea of a 'chain of oligopolies' defined in terms of consumer preferences.[2] Meanwhile Joan Robinson followed Sraffa in seeing reality as 'a world of monopolies' and it seemed indeed as though monopoly 'released from its uncomfortable pen' had 'swallowed up the competitive analysis' of both the firm and the industry.[3]

Recent theories of the firm (behavioural theory, managerial capitalism, sales-revenue maximisation, etc.) are all really theories of the 'giant producer' where the interest is focused on the firm's internal organisational structure. The theories may be formally stated as appropriate to

35

'oligopoly', but competitive interdependence between businesses is hardly discussed; the firm is seen as large enough to control its own destiny, and it is assumed to have an individual determinate demand curve.

Analysis of the 'industry' has thus effectively gone, except in the very special case of perfect competition. But surely 'monopoly' is just as much a special case? If we are concerned with price theory, we need to be able to handle business groups of different sizes down to only a few producers competing with homogeneous or differentiated products. Our theory needs to be rooted in a theory of the firm, because the process of costing-up its products take place within the firm and it is the firm which quotes a price to a customer. But the price which is actually quoted will also reflect the price *policy* of the firm, and to understand that, we need to know the competitive forces to which it is subject. Thus, in quoting for a tender in the building industry, the price arrived at by costings is subjected to a further process of 'evaluation' by top management; and the price quoted for a water-tube boiler contract reflects the manufacturer's estimate of the favourableness of his position on this work relative to others likely to quote. During tendering, the process of weighing up the competition is likely to be made explicit, but it is present in all pricing decisions whenever there is an alternative to the one supplier. In other words, it is exceptional for a firm to be 'an island'; a realistic theory of the firm needs to be integrated with a concept of the industry, and the forces working at that level, before we can understand, for example, the determination of price, and the profitability of firms.

INDUSTRY AND MARKET

The concept of the industry should focus our analysis on the supply side. We have created difficulties for ourselves by not distinguishing between an industry and a market. Again, on the very simplifying assumptions of a homogeneous product and single-product firms, there was no need to make a distinction, and in perfect competition 'industry' and 'market' come to the same thing. But in more realistic conditions it seems useful to separate out the concepts. Let us here keep the term market for the product demand side and the term industry for the product supply side. The Andrewsian definition of an industry runs in terms of common techniques and processes:

> ... an individual business must be conceived as operating within an 'industry' which consists of all businesses which operate processes of a sufficiently similar kind (which implies the possession of substantially similar technical resources) and possessing sufficiently similar back-

grounds of experience and knowledge so that each of them could produce the particular commodity under consideration, and would do so if it were sufficiently attractive.[4]

In other words, we are concerned here with manufacturing substitution of product. And the grouping of firms which is relevant are those which could produce the product over any time period with which we are concerned. The market is a narrower concept, because it is related to the product demand curve which must be more narrowly specific, even if we recognise it as a statistical demand curve covering different grades and qualities of a product. In considering the market, we are concerned with consumer substitution. For example, we might say that there is a demand and a market for each of the categories of trousers, sports jackets, suits etc., and that these will be supplied by the men's clothing industry. There is a demand and a market for each of climbing boots, sandals, dress shoes etc., and these will be supplied by the boot and shoe industry.[5]

One could presumably think of instances where the market and the industry are coterminous, but analytically we should be able to keep them apart. To take some cases that may seem difficult: a consumer's need for a container or wrapping might be supplied by a metal box, a glass jar or a plastic film, and, in this sense, the can, glass and plastic producers may be in competition with each other. But they remain, in my terminology, in separate industries, although their products are consumer substitutes in this case. For this particular use, different industries are in the same market; in sub-markets within this broad class (e.g. milk containers) one or the other industry may have such a comparative advantage as to exclude the other industries from competition; a large firm producing both glass and tin containers I would analyse as being in two separate industries.

Let us consider by-product production; I would say that the producers of by-product sulphate of ammonia are not in the same industry as the producers of synthetic ammonia although they are in the same product market; this is because the by-product producers are coke-oven plants which produce ammonia incidentally, there is no cost of production in any normal sense (though there would be a cost of disposal of the poisonous ammonia if it were not fixed in the form of sulphate), and the supply is determined by the demand for coke. The synthetic ammonia industry will have to take the supply of the by-product producers into account, because they cannot be knocked out of the market, but their supply is inelastic with respect to the price of ammonia, so may be taken as given, and for any output greater than that it is the competition of synthetic producers which is relevant.

Another example of difficulties is shown up when considering iron and steel production: here we have two groups of producers, the large integrated steel firms and the makers of iron and steel products who do not make ingot steel. Here I would suggest we are considering two different industries, one of which has more producers than the other:[6] the large integrated firms *can* produce most products, so will be in the iron and steel products industry as well as the iron and steel industry. But in the case of a product such as sheet steel, this can only be produced by the large integrated firm, so the industry in this case must be differently defined if we assume that the re-rollers, for instance, would not normally be able to integrate backwards. Similarly, the aluminium industry is distinct from the secondary aluminium products industry, but a number of firms will be in both industries, either actually or potentially.

ENTRY COMPETITION

An industry is therefore that grouping of firms which is in competition with each other in the sense of any firm being able to produce a commodity with the same technical specifications and, we must add, being able to sell it in competition with the product of other firms. I suggest that competition is much more pervasive in practice than the 'large firm' theories imply. Doubt about the force of competition in oligopoly has been expressed perhaps most strongly by Galbraith. He has stated that the faith in competition as a self-generating regulatory mechanism was destroyed 'after a market had been pre-empted by a few large sellers, after entry of new firms had become difficult, and after existing firms had accepted a convention against price competition'; and again 'In the market of small numbers or oligopoly, the practical barriers to entry and the convention against price competition have eliminated the self-generating capacity of competition.'[7] But every term in this indictment is suspect. In the first place, competition takes place not at the level of the firm but at the product level. All businesses are multi-product; the largest producer of any one product is not necessarily the largest business in the industry, and the identity of the largest producer will probably change from product to product within the industry. (For example, in the U.K. soap and detergent industry, Procter and Gamble is the largest producer of detergent powders, but Unilever is the largest producer of soap powders, and neither is the dominant firm in liquid detergents. If one extends this analysis to all the other products they produce, from shampoos to oilcake, the range of competitive relationships becomes enormous.)

Secondly, I suggest that entry is much easier and will come more quickly than Galbraith supposes. His analysis assumes that entry comes

only from 'new firms'. This is also true of Bain's analysis of barriers to
competition where new entrants are defined as new legal entities installing
new capacity.[8] This would appear to go back to static pure-competition
analysis, with the marginal firm waiting in the wings, as it were, smaller,
more ignorant, less efficient than firms already established in the industry.
But Andrews has pointed out the importance of cross-entry competition,
i.e. firms already established in other product markets who can move into
this market. These may be firms in quite a different industry which are
seeking diversification. It may be a firm integrating backwards to control
its supply of materials, or integrating forward to control its immediate
market. It may be a firm already in the same industry, but moving into a
market which it was not in before. Thus, entry to any particular product is
as likely to come from an established medium-sized or large firm as it is to
come from the small new firm starting from scratch. In this case, the
barriers to entry distinguished by Bain, for instance, are likely to become
negligible — existing established firms have as easy access to finance, have
an established reputation which can be capitalised on in other markets,
have scale economies already and the possibility of exploiting joint costs,
etc. And entry in these circumstances can take place quickly.

An unjustified limitation of analysis of entry competition follows from
the Bain/Galbraith assumptions about barriers to new entry. A case study
which shows such limitations is that by Martin of the U.S. chlorine—alkali
industry in which he employs Bain's model and concludes that there has
been no entry to the industry in spite of three decades of expansion for
the industry and relatively low barriers. Yet, on the facts reported in his
own article, he records 'invasion [of the end-use products markets] by
extension of product lines'. The fact that this has come about, on the one
hand, by forward integration by chlorine producers and, on the other, by
other chemical companies moving into these products puts it outside the
Bain definition of entry. But nonetheless this should not lead us to deny
the reality of new competition. Martin also records an increase in chemical
companies undertaking their own captive production of chlorine, so that
only 40 per cent of chlorine produced was sold in 1954, as against 65 per
cent in 1937. These firms might well be considered entrants to the
chlorine industry: they would have had the alternative of buying chlorine
from the existing producers, and because they make it for themselves the
market for the existing producers is eaten into by that amount. The really
interesting phenomenon appears to me to be that they have not invaded
the independent chlorine market; thus price has apparently been low
enough to forestall entry into the free market but not into the captive
market for chlorine, and one can think of reasons why this might be so.[9]

Further, let us look at the treatment of product differentiation and advertising in Bain's approach. Bain considers differentiation to be the most important barrier to entry. Firstly, I have already made the point that if entry comes from an established firm in another industry it may still have a 'household name' which is equally acceptable to consumers as any other brand name existing in this market. Secondly, we tend to think too much in terms of consumer buyers: a high percentage of goods are in fact sold to other producers – machinery and tools, raw materials, semi-finished goods, etc. Even final consumer goods will go through wholesale and retail channels composed of business buyers who must be assumed knowledgeable and reasonably skilled at their job. Thirdly, differentiation of product may facilitate entry as much as hindering it. Looked at from the manufacturer's side, differentiation of product is a way *into* a market, finding the niche which is not already filled, producing a product which is that much better or more convenient for some uses than the products of others. More generally, the whole of this analysis has been too dominated by looking only at the consumer-substitution, product-market side. Advertising, similarly, is not just a question of persuading the consumer to purchase brand X rather than brand Y – a market gained solely by persuasive advertising is as easily lost to another persuader. Advertising has a function in terms of the structure of an industry. From the manufacturer's point of view, it is a means of introducing a new product, getting it tried by consumers (and thereafter a consumer may judge the product for himself). Advertising may be used to help the standardisation of output and so to get longer production runs and lower costs. It may be used to persuade retailers to stock the product in the places and in the quantities desired. For some products (some of the most heavily advertised consumer goods, e.g. toothpaste), *all* firms have to advertise if they are to be in the market at all, and advertising will simply maintain each firm's approximate share of the market and give relative stability in inherently unstable markets. There will be an appropriate norm of advertising for a particular industry, and increased advertising will not in itself give the power to increase prices. Of course, in this case the threshold cost of advertising may give pause, but this is in a different category to differentiation itself being a barrier.

If entry is relatively easy, if the competitive grouping of firms changes with every product, it is not easy to accept Galbraith's view that there is a 'convention against price competition' as the general case. (Of course, I am not arguing that there are not such cases of non-competition to be found.)

We must here explicitly bring in time. All I have said so far is that we are concerned with that grouping of firms which *could* produce the product over any time period with which we are concerned. In the short run this is the existing manufacturers who are already in the product market and have the necessary production and marketing set-up. Ask any manufacturer who his main competitors are, and he will tell you, by name. But in the long run there are many more who could produce the product. In the very long run, of course, there is no limitation, in the sense that capital and management are non-specific and entry may come from anywhere; but this is the long run when, to quote Keynes, 'we are all dead'. The long run with which I am concerned, and with which businessmen are concerned in their policy, is much shorter than that. I have tried to show that entry is much easier and may come more quickly than most economic analysis allows. Of course, one can think of exceptions, for example where very specific plant is needed which takes a long time to build, or when a specific distribution or service network has to be built up. But, starting at the firm level and gradually widening one's horizon, one can analyse in each case the widening circles of competition and potential competition, and where there is a gap which will make the pressure less. To take the example of a producer of fitted women's shoes: his immediate competitors will be those (few) other firms who also produce fitted women's shoes in his price range, and he will know precisely who those firms are and what their comparative advantages are; the next circle of competitors will be those who produce similar shoes in slightly lower or slightly better quality; the next circle may be more fashionable but less fitted shoes in a similar price range, or less fashionable but as fitted shoes in a cheaper price range; the next circle may be the producers of boys' and girls' shoes; the next the producers of men's shoes who also make ladies' walking shoes; and so on, until all the boot and shoe industry is included. The composition of any circle of competition will depend on the firm which is taken as starting point. The concept is parallel to Chamberlin's idea of a 'chain of oligopolies', but the reader must always remember that we are concerned with producer substitution, not consumer substitution, of product when talking about industry or oligopoly.

PRODUCT AND PRICE
In the long run, no business will be able to get a higher price than any other business would charge for a technically identical product as delivered to the particular customer. Prices will thus reflect normal costs,[10] through the competition of producers as much as through the discrimination of consumers. In an established industry with established products, prices for different varieties of the product will bear a definite cost-equivalence to each other. The costing-up rules which a business employs tend to bring

this about automatically if its position is normally competitive and it can use its own costs as a guide to others' costs. If it is too small to have the major economies of scale, or is inefficient, or trying to establish itself in what is a new market for it, it will not be able to 'get its price'.[11] Procedures may be more or less refined, but may be generalised into the calculation of the level of average direct costs and the adding to this of some allowance for overhead costs and net profit. The prices entering into average direct costs – the rates paid to labour and the price of raw materials – are approximately common for all businesses in the industry. If there are changes in these input prices therefore, the price of the product will be adjusted correspondingly, since all businesses are affected and their relative competitive position is unchanged. Similarly, the gross profit margin will cover the normal overhead costs of dealing with this product, but the size of the total gross profit margin, what it is 'safe' to charge, will be determined by the competition which is actually or potentially present in the market and which sets the ceiling to price. If a firm is 'normally' competitive on this product its net profit will be normal; if it is in an individually weak position, net profit will be minimal or non-existent. The firm which is particularly strong – either because it has exceptionally low costs or exceptional product-acceptance – may show higher than normal net profit, or it may show higher than normal overhead costs, for example it may choose to pay its managers exceptionally high salaries. But it must be confident that this abnormally strong position is a true long-run one, i.e. that it can charge the 'rent' of its unique economies of scale or its exceptional market power.

To take some practical instances which have been in the news lately: the rise in the price of cars which has taken place in 1973–4 even in a falling market, reflects the fact that costs have risen for *all* car manu-facturers, and they are confident that the higher price in present circum-stances will not bring in any other competitor. The high profits that Kelloggs have been shown to make is not because there is no competition – apart from other manufacturers of breakfast foods, large retailing chains such as Spar have been attracted to put their own house brand of cornflakes on sale in their shops at a lower price than Kelloggs – and the lack of success of these other brands appears to show that Kelloggs *can* charge a rent because it is considered by consumers to be a superior product. One can think of other firms who have simply made a mistake in pricing, and as a result lost market share,[12] or become so unprofitable that they have been subjected to take-over.[13] There seems to be some evidence that the first effects of an inflationary boom may be to squeeze profits, as firms are reluctant to raise price sufficiently, or sufficiently quickly, in case their competitors are better placed than they are. But as the realisation spreads that inflation is becoming very rapid, that all prices are rising (both factor input prices and other product prices) that there is shortage of capacity, that demand is not choked off and customers *expect* rising prices, then firms may become greedy, and a general shake-out may be necessary before conditions become 'normal' again.

An assumption in the argument is that businesses are primarily interested in their long-run position in normal price decisions. This is partly because a manufacturer has sunk a good deal in investment which will take time to justify itself; and partly because the long run in actual time may come relatively shortly. Existing businesses will normally have spare capacity and will gladly accept extra orders at a price which is no lower than they are getting already, and new competitors will come more quickly than if one assumes only the entry and slow growth of absolutely new firms. Moreover, a customer lost through a high-price policy is not so easily regained. So an entry-preventing price policy is the sensible thing for an entrepreneur who wishes to maximise his return over any period longer than a day or so.

In terms of static analysis, we can therefore hark back to the old concept of 'an industry' and analyse it as though it were producing a cost-equivalent standard commodity. Following Andrews's theory of the firm, given stable demand will be supplied at a normal cost price. Extensions to that demand will be met in the short run by increased supplies at the same price, and in the long run at decreased price (*ceteris paribus*).

Andrews's theory, however, is not simply static. In practice, of course, firms are in a dynamic world. The realistic form that competition takes is a continual probing of the market by firms, increasing output of that product which looks more profitable, modifying design, shifting emphasis in response to actions of competitors and to pressures from customers, which again reflect actions or non-actions of competitors. But this only makes it more sure that the price limit that a firm can get is set by the costs at which another manufacturer could supply. One meaning implicit in our delineation of the industry in terms of the supply side is that a firm has the knowledge, for any product, to calculate the average direct costs of production and hence the size of the gross profit margin at any given price. If the gross profit margin looks attractive compared with that which the firm is getting on the range of products it is currently producing, that is a signal for further investigation and possible entry.

In practice, again, we must recognise the importance of innovation in getting the edge over competitors. Even putting on one side major technological change or major new-use products, which to some extent are random in their incidence, we should recognise the continuous innovational product changes going on all the time, which are under the control of the firm. Profit margins can be higher on a new product, and some firms will rely on a constant stream of 'new' products, in this minor sense, to get an adequate average profit overall. With a revolutionary new product, a policy of low price and building up the market long run may be more likely.[14]

This is only to touch on the endless varieties of relationships which are possible within one industry. In any case, what we observe in practice is not equilibrium conditions. Not all firms at any one time need to be making profits even if there appears to be an equilibrium of industrial price. Some small firms will be new entrants, hanging on and hoping to grow by special merits and endeavours to a position of practicable optimum scale. Other firms, left behind in the race, will be on their way out. But the condition of exit is not the same as the condition of entry. Exit may be a very long-drawn-out process; there is the example of the firm making locomotives in the inter-war years which only made book profits in one or two years after 1921 but was still in existence in 1938. Larger, more aggressive firms will not be able to drive from the market those businesses which are already on a sufficient scale to have paying-out (cash) costs which are no higher than the average total costs of the larger firms. They will be able at least to survive at any prices which will give an adequate return to the larger businesses.[15]

Again, the *actual* level of costs (as distinct from the theoretical possibilities inherent in the LRAC curve) will depend on historical factors at any given moment. A firm first in the market may for a time have peculiar advantages, either in economies of scale or in market acceptance. But later, in production costs it may suffer Veblen's 'penalty of the pioneer', so that improvements in technology may enable an entrant to come in with a plant on a newer, lower level of costs, and compete with the larger firm even if it is at less than optimum scale.[16] The change in technology will lead to instability, and a new equilibrium price has to be determined at a lower level in real terms. The actual time it takes for the first firm to get its costs and prices down may be enough to allow the newcomer to grow to practicable optimum size. In any case, the former firm is unlikely to be able to knock the latter out, for the reasons given in the preceding paragraph.

While firms may be active potential competitors, there will be differences between them in the number of products produced and in the type of products. Each firm will tend to specialise on what it does best. In this way complementary relationships between businesses may be as important as directly competitive ones. The large firm may go for large-scale operation of the basic processes and those products which require quantity production. Smaller firms will have their own advantages in speciality products which require very special care in their manufacture or very special attention to the time and manner of meeting their customers' wants. The smaller firm may supply the odd need for quick delivery, perhaps of a varied range of specifications. It will not be Courtaulds who supplies the occasional beam of experimental material. It will not be Guest, Keen and Nettlefolds who supplies a small number of screws of peculiar specifications. The small or medium-sized firm may be selling regionally not nationally, and, since the major technical economies of scale probably go with plant size rather than firm size, it may be a match in that region for any branch of a larger firm (large firms typically having many plants, operated in different districts). The smaller firm may not try to be the initiator in any sense, but will ride in later on the back of the larger firm's effort, either in research or in advertising.

In this way the small and the large firm are often in different markets. But if they are in the same industry, as I have defined it, they remain potential competitors in the long run. There will be cross-checks, on costs and prices, between firms in the same industry. Thus the car manufacturer buys certain components from specialist accessory manufacturers who can get greater economies of scale by supplying all car manufacturers than any one of the latter can achieve; but the car manufacturer often makes *some* of the components himself and would at once make more if he thought he could do it at a lower price. The large building firm will still keep a small works department because of the interconnexions of all types of building work. There are often two-way relationships: the producers of the final products buying the intermediate goods which come from the basic processers, and perhaps selling back the final product to the latter. Thus Guest, Keen and Nettlefolds supplies blanks to small screwmakers and, as I have indicated, may buy odd lots of screws from such firms instead of disrupting its own flow production to make them. Re-rollers in steel buy from the integrated heavy steel industry, which in some cases factors their products.

In a dynamic world there will be constant shifts in firms' positions in individual product markets. There will not, however, be constant shifts in price. Short run, we may explain this by the 'kinked demand curve' which itself does bring in the reactions of competitors. But this only tells us why price is not changed in the short run and does not explain the determination of price itself. For this, I suggest that we need a theory of pragmatic long-run profit maximisation, through entry-preventing price policy. Andrews's normal-cost theory provides this. Further, it is not enough for analysis to remain at the level of the firm; we need to place that firm in the setting of forces which operate at the industry level. If we look again at the concepts of 'entry', 'differentiation of product' etc., and if we define the industry from the supply side, we get a very different view of the forces of competition than is given in recent theories of the firm. It is time that we reinstated the theory of competitive industry as a possible tool of analysis even when handling 'oligopoly' situations.

# 4 The Water Tube Boilermakers' Association Agreement and Trial

INTRODUCTORY NOTE

The proof of evidence of P. W. S. Andrews tendered on behalf of the Water Tube Boilermakers' Association in the Restrictive Practices Court[1] may be considered a self-contained document in that it analyses the economic characteristics of the industry, and the present and likely future circumstances of the industry, before discussing the working of the agreement. I have included, as an appendix, the note he also submitted to the Court, when proofs had been exchanged, on the proof of evidence of Professor Pool, the economist called by the Registrar. Professor Pool's proof was largely concerned with rebutting the respondents' claims as set forth in their Statement of Case and discusses the price restrictions from the point of view of general economic theory. He laid no claim to first-hand knowledge of the industry – and, indeed, made it something of a point of principle not to have met and talked with any boilermakers (*Transcript of Proceedings*, Day 9, pp. 51–2). The difference in type of proof is partly due to the different role of anyone appearing for the respondents, on whom lies the onus of proof and who have to prove the 'exceptional' nature of their case, and that of the Registrar, who need not do more than rehearse a general presumption; but partly it is also due to Philip Andrews's particular approach to industry which involved him getting to understand it from the inside.

Readers may like to be reminded, as background, that the W.T.B.A. case was the fifth reference to be heard by the Restrictive Practices Court, the hearings taking place June–July 1959, and was the first to be won by the respondents. The agreement to be defended had only been introduced in February 1957, having succeeded a more restrictive price and market-sharing agreement. The new agreement had been devised in the light of the Restrictive Trade Practices Act 1956 to be minimally restrictive and yet give the members what was essential and justifiable, as they thought. It was not a price agreement, in the sense that each firm determined its own price for its own reasons independently of any other firm. But when an inquiry went to more than one member, if it related to home trade or to certain export markets (mainly the Commonwealth, excluding Canada) those members who had received the inquiry met together just before submitting their bids, under the independent chairmanship of the director of the Association. This meeting would first decide who would be the 'selected member', and then the prices, previously sent in to the director, would be 'tabled'. The prices would then be 'evaluated' on a common basis, 'material for material and performance for performance', and so the 'lowest evaluated price' would be arrived at. Only the selected member could alter his price after the prices had been tabled, and, if he were not the lowest, he had the choice of coming down wholly or in part to the lowest evaluated price, but not below it.

The Judgment has been attacked by commentators for its 'inconsistencies',[2] In fact, *any* judgment which the Court has given in favour of the respondents has been attacked by some economist arguing that the judgment is based on faulty reasoning.[3] To someone who has sat through all the hearings in a case the Judgment takes on a different aspect. It appears essentially as a legal decision, influenced, for example, very considerably by the credibility of witnesses in the box, couched in whatever form is most convenient legally, for example that form which will most easily avoid appeal, the justice of the final result being the important thing rather than the consistency of parts.[4] Since there is no appeal on facts, only on law, from this Court, there is a natural tendency to pronounce factually rather than legally wherever possible. And there is a natural wish to avoid setting legal precedents which could hamper later cases. One may, of course, argue that the matter to be tried is not really justifiable and that it is a matter for economists and economic reasoning.[5] But then one should really be critical of submitting such matter to Court procedure rather than critical of the judgments as pieces of economic analysis.

On the economics side of the W.T.B.A. case, Registrar's counsel chose to make his major assault on Philip Andrews's proof in cross-examination by attacking the whole idea that the industry was currently in a recession, which was likely to get worse, before demand picked up in the long term when all the capacity at present employed in the industry would be needed. Counsel's argument was that the present slight dip was simply a return to 'normality' and 'the normal level' of trading (*Transcript of Proceedings*, Day 7, p. 32) after an artificially high peak for the ten years following the war – 'a pause for consolidation after the momentum of the post-war years' (Day 7, p. 41). Counsel returned again and again to this point, and to trying to get Andrews to estimate precisely how long he thought the 'recession' would last. As a partisan observer, I had no doubt that the tactical victory had gone to Andrews. The battle, however, was really won the next day, when the main witness for the Registrar went into the box, Mr L. F. Miller, chief purchasing and contracts officer of the Central Electricity Generating Board. In cross-examination, step by step, Mr Miller agreed to the following figures:[6]

| As at 31 March | Generating plant under construction or planned in the U.K. | | No. of boilers |
|---|---|---|---|
| 1955 | to end of 1960 | | 210 |
| 1956 | 1961 | | 166 |
| 1957 | 1962 | | 91 |
| 1959 | 1964 | estimates (maximum) | 83 |
| 1960 | 1965 | | 59 |
| 1961 | 1966 | | 46 |
| 1962 | 1967 | | 34 |

At the end, when asked to check the figures, Mr Miller said quite frankly 'I would think, without even checking these figures, that the conclusion is correct', the figures are 'of the right order', and 'I entirely agree — I am putting it as plainly as I can — that the boilermakers are at the moment in a position of difficulty' (Day 8, p. 55). This admission 'against his own side' as it would be seen, would be conclusive to the legal mind, and enabled the Judgment to say, unblushingly, 'The unchallenged evidence was that the industry is now in a position of difficulty' (L.R. 1 R.P. at p. 327).

The Judgment, when it is rehearsing the facts, largely adopts the view that will be found in Andrews's proof — of a technologically advanced industry, rapidly changing, with high paying-out overhead costs, important research, large and efficient firms, short-term excess capacity but long-term demand likely to exceed capacity. '... we are satisfied that it would not be in the national interest that any of these member companies should be forced by economic pressure to give up boiler production' (L.R. 1 R.P. at p. 329). The Court also expressed itself as satisfied that the scheme was 'honestly worked'. (L.R. 1 R.P. at p. 334), that the prices were 'really competitive and keen ... by which we mean prices which cover overheads and depreciation and allow a small, but only very reasonable, margin of profit' (L.R. 1 R.P. at p. 334), and that the scheme brought the members advantages.

The Act is, of course, concerned with the public interest. The respondents pleaded three of the 'gateways' provided by the various paragraphs of Section 21 (1) of the Act. Paragraph (b) required them to prove 'that the removal of the restriction would deny to the public ... specific and substantial benefits ...', and the Court found against them.

While agreeing that it was vital to the companies to preserve capacity in the form of key personnel, and maintain research and quality, the Court concluded that the companies were well aware of this vital necessity and would therefore keep these personnel and activities in any case, and as large companies of good financial standing they could afford to do this over 'the next four or five years' and 'take advantage of the gradual return to full demand which we expect to occur after that period' (L.R. 1 R.P. at p. 337).

Paragraph (d) of Section 21 (1) requires respondents to prove 'that the restriction is reasonably necessary ... to negotiate fair terms for the supply of goods to ... any person ... who ... controls a preponderant part of the market for such goods.' Here the Court's judgment was that the case had been proved: the Electricity Board placed 83 per cent of the total home orders and 56 per cent of the combined home and overseas orders for 1952–8, so it was clearly a preponderant buyer; and the Court held that it was not necessary to prove that the Board was likely to try to enforce unfair terms – it was sufficient that in the circumstances of the industry 'the suppliers will not be enabled to negotiate fair terms, but in the hope of getting an occasional contract are likely to tender at uneconomic prices' (L.R. 1 R.P. at 341). However, the justification under paragraph (d) failed because the restriction was 'quite unnecessarily wide' – 'for the simple reason that it applies not only to contracts with the Electricity Board but to all other contracts for home industrial boilers and all contracts of every kind situate in a large number of overseas territories' (L.R. 1 R.P. at p. 341).

Paragraph (f) contains the export gateway – 'that ... the removal of the restriction would be likely to cause a reduction in the volume or earnings of the export business which is substantial ...' This was the gateway through which the respondents passed. The Court held that, given the increasing size of boilers 'the loss in any year of even one overseas contract may represent a substantial reduction in the export figures of the industry' (L.R. 1 R.P. at p. 345). And it declared '... we do believe in fact that the continued existence of the rule will enable the members to obtain a larger share of overseas orders (which cannot be numerous) than would be the case if the restriction was abolished' (L.R. 1 R.P. at p. 343). The facts given to support this belief were that there was greater exchange of technical knowledge and know-how than in the case of home orders, and that in choosing the selected member greater emphasis was placed on customer preference and less upon the record of trading. This operation of the agreement in the export field meant that there was more likelihood of achieving the lowest price in line with the general level of prices, and 'the combination of customer preference and the lowest price must help to secure overseas business'. In addition, the agreement meant more likelihood of staffs and local offices being kept in existence overseas.

On the balancing of advantage and detriments under the 'tailpiece' to Section 21 (1) of the Act of 1956, the Court found that the only real detriment of the scheme was that 'the purchasers of boilers might have to pay rather more than they otherwise would for their boilers' (L.R. 1 R.P. at p. 346). This detriment was held not to outweigh the national benefit resulting from the maintenance of exports. There is a very interesting passage, however, where the Court deals with other detriments alleged by the Registrar, summarised as follows: 'The first two grounds allege that the effect of the restriction is to prevent or restrict the free play of competition between firms of differing efficiency and that the scheme for influencing the distribution of contracts tends to prevent the concentration of business on the low-cost boilermakers and involves an uneconomical use of the nation's productive resources' (L.R. 1 R.P. at pp. 345–6). The Judgment, as delivered, goes on positively to reject these submissions: 'We have already given our reasons for not accepting these submissions, in the special circumstances of this case, when we were considering paragraph (d). We think it is in the national interest to preserve existing capacity in this special case.' The Judgment as recorded in L.R. 1 R.P. (at p. 346) however, is different: 'We have already given our reasons for not accepting the first of these submissions, in the special circumstances of this case, when we were considering paragraph (d). As to the second, as we have already stated, we are satisfied that with or without the scheme there will be no reduction of capacity in the industry.' The Court appears to have had second thoughts; it no longer declares it beneficial to preserve existing capacity but simply argues that it does not need to decide the question since there will be no reduction of capacity anyway.

This shows, perhaps the great difficulties faced by the Court in the form of any Judgment. To a layman, it appeared that the Court made up its mind on the case as a whole, paying more attention to facts, such as the actual good export record of the industry, than to any economic argument which it might consider 'hypothetical'. Its judgment does not have to be consistent in terms of economic argument, only in legal terms. Having made up its mind, it then considered each of the gateways relied upon by the industry. The gateway provided for by paragraph (b) was rejected, possibly because it was so general. The gateway provided for by paragraph (d) was rejected on technical grounds, but if the respondents had not won a victory in substance under paragraph (d), they would almost certainly have run into substantial problems when, having passed through the gateway provided for by paragraph (*f*), they reached the 'tailpiece' to Section 21 (1). Paragraph (*f*) raised fewest difficulties. The need for exports was one thing all men might be considered agreed on, and there could be few industries which could claim, as the W.T.B.A., that the loss of even one contract might represent the loss of £1 million foreign exchange.

PROOF OF EVIDENCE
of
PHILIP WALTER SAWFORD ANDREWS
*TENDERED ON BEHALF OF THE RESPONDENTS*
PHILIP WALTER SAWFORD ANDREWS will say:

1. I am an Official Fellow of Nuffield College and a university lecturer in the University of Oxford and am also general editor of the *Journal of Industrial Economics*. Besides other publications, I am author of *Manufacturing Business*, joint editor of and contributor to *Oxford Studies in the Price Mechanism*, and joint author of *Capital Development in Steel*, an economic study of the United Steel Companies Ltd, as well as of the *Life of Lord Nuffield*.

2. I am a member of the Economics Committee and the Human Sciences Committee of the Department of Scientific and Industrial Research; also of the Building Research Board and of its Economics and Industrial Operations Sub-committee. I was a member of the official United Kingdom delegation to the European Productivity Administration's Conference on Automation in 1957.

3. For nearly twenty-five years I have specialised in research into the economics of individual businesses. For the past five years I have made some studies of restrictive practices in manufacturing industry, including the life history of an international cartel.

4. I had some acquaintance with the water-tube boilermaking industry from the customer's end, since some of the industries I have studied generate electricity as part of their operations. But I had made no special study of the industry before I was invited by the Water Tube Boilermakers' Association to prepare an opinion on the economic aspects of their case.

5. The Association's Statement of Case had been delivered before I was asked to give my opinions. The Association has given me facilities for independent inquiry so far as time has allowed and I have visited the works of the largest and smallest producers of water-tube boilers among the members of the Association. I was able to go round the largest works with an official delegation from the Russian electrical power industry, to which I shall make reference later on.

6. I was interested when I received the invitation, to reflect that I had had no complaints about the operation of any agreement between members of this Association. I have generally found that businessmen, even though they may be organised in price fixing or other restrictive associations themselves, are usually very ready to suspect a 'racket' on the part of suppliers' associations. In this connection I refer to a copy of a reply which Messrs Courtaulds Ltd, a large industrial customer of the Association, sent to a questionnaire from the Registrar arising out of the present case, which copy Messrs Courtaulds sent to the Association. In this reply this customer said that they had 'ordered watertube boiler plant during approximately the last five years', inviting tenders from both Association and independent boilermakers and in one case from Germany (but in the event the German firms did not tender), that they had no reason for being dissatisfied with prices quoted and thought they were competitive, that they did not consider they suffered any detriment as a result of the W.T.B.A. agreement and their general view was that 'the efficiency of the plant offered, and the honesty of tender and the co-operation of the supplier in order to give the customer what he wants are good. In our view these considerations are more important than any marginal price differences'.

7. I also refer to some remarks which Lord Citrine is reported to have made in 1954. Since he was Chairman of the British Electricity Authority from 1948 until 1957, I attach importance to the fact that he had 'very little complaint to make' about the supplying industries in general of which the water-tube boilermaking industry is an important part:

> If I had to compare British industry and American industry, I would say that British industry is very much less in its practices a menace to the public interest. With regard to our own position vis-a-vis industry, we have very little complaint to make. We make our direct representations to the associations concerned, and we are always conscious of two things. The first is that unrestricted competition cannot be ultimately in the interests of anybody. That may seem a curious statement to make, but competition ought to be based first of all upon fair standards. . . . Secondly, in modern industry a fair price margin is essential to the carrying on of the industry. . . .[7]

I refer later, paragraph 51, to another matter raised by Lord Citrine on that occasion which appears to be relevant to another aspect of this case.

8. In my evidence I shall confine myself to the economic aspects of the tendering arrangements operated by the Association, and to the factual matters which I consider of relevance to its case. I begin by stating what I

think are the fundamental characteristics of the industry and the position of the members of the Association within it. I shall then consider the circumstances facing the industry at the present time and in the foreseeable future. After that I shall be in a position to explain the working of the agreement as regards tendering arrangements. I shall then state the benefits which I think follow from the working of the agreement in this industry and in the circumstances I shall have described. I shall also consider the detriments which might conceivably result from the agreement including those which the Registrar alleges.

ECONOMIC CHARACTERISTICS OF THE INDUSTRY
The Nature of the Product

9. The water-tube boiler is the predominant method of raising steam for large-scale electrical generation. For smaller-scale production of steam and smaller-scale generation of electricity as a by-product of process and waste heat, there are competitive methods of steam raising.

10. In industries (such as rayon, chemicals or paper) where large quantities of steam are required for regular processes, large businesses will often find it economical to generate at least part of their own electricity with plant involving a water-tube boiler installation.

11. For central authority work, the water-tube boiler is the basis of the conventional thermal generation of electricity. It has proved capable of continuous development in size and towards higher temperatures and pressures. Table 1 [see end of chapter] shows the increasing size of generating sets programmed. The 550,000 kW set at Thorpe Marsh, planned for operation in 1963 'will have a greater electrical output than the whole' of the present Battersea Power Station' (*Central Electricity Report and Accounts*, 1957–8, para. 108).

12. Alongside the increased size of set has occurred an even greater relative increase in the size of boilers. Whereas previously several boilers served one or more generating sets with arrangements, involving spare boiler capacity, to take care of maintenance, etc., it has been possible thanks to improved design to develop the 'unit-type' system in which all the steam for one generating set comes from a single boiler.[8] More, boiler size has proved capable of development beyond the limitations governing the sizes of alternators and the Thorpe Marsh installation referred to in paragraph 11 will supply a twin generating set from its single boiler. Not only are modern boilers larger in size, thus economising in plant housing, controls, etc., they are generally worked at higher temperatures and pressures with a more elaborate system of control arrangements to ensure reliability and continuity of service. It may be noted that the modern

reheat system, the adoption of which has been made possible by advances in boiler design (so that unit-type boilers may be used despite the more strenuous working conditions to which they will be subjected), has given boilers a practical energy output which is correspondingly higher than implied by the conventional rating in terms of lb of steam an hour. In one way or another, the consequence of modern design developments has been a considerable saving in fuel costs and a saving in capital costs per unit of electricity produced which offset for the customer any tendency towards increased cost of the more elaborate boiler plant reckoned on the basis of nominal evaporation capacity.[9]

13. As regards saving in fuel costs, the C.E.A. *Report and Accounts for 1956–57* (para. 216) shows that in the nine years 1949–57 31,441,000 tons of coal were saved through increased thermal efficiency. At the same time, the 'capital costs of conventional power stations commissioned in 1948 and those under construction in 1957' has remained constant at an average of £50 per kilowatt installed: 'In face of an overall increase in the 9¾ years of some 70 per cent in the prices of materials and wage rates.' (C.E. *Report and Accounts*, 1957–8, para. 19).

14. An illustration of the long-term changes so far as boilers are concerned is given in the chairman's speech at the annual general meeting of John Thompson, Ltd, in 1957:

> Only thirty years ago the average boiler being installed in power stations in Britain was designed to evaporate 100,000 lb of steam an hour. Today John Thompson is building single units generating more than 860,000 lb an hour. In that same span of years the steam pressure employed in the boilers has increased from 325 to 1600 lb p.s.i., and power station thermal efficiencies have been increased by some 50 per cent.

15. Table 2 analyses C.E.A. and C.E.G.B. orders placed in 1951–7 to show directly the increase in the average size of boilers ordered, particularly since 1953. It also shows the difference between members and non-members in respect of the average size of boilers to which I shall want to refer later. Here, however, I am concerned only with the general pattern of the industry.

16. The British electrical power-generating industry has, of course, played its part in the stimulation of design and development of generating equipment, and since the nationalisation of the industry the Central Electricity Authority has played a central role in modern developments. With claims to early inventions in their own field, W.T.B.A. members have

been partners in, and helped to originate these developments and the reports of the Authority contain frequent if anonymous recognition of this (e.g. 1957–8 *Report*, paras 102 and 105). A number of them are now concerned as partners in the several atomic energy consortia, where, since steam has so far proved the most convenient way of converting nuclear heat to electrical energy, the large-scale technology of water-tube boiler manufacturers makes an important contribution.

17. A water-tube boiler is typically bought as part of a larger installation. But the specialised knowledge and experience ('know-how') and the peculiarities of the boiler installation itself has led to its supply continuing to develop as a separate industry. Manufacture involves the design of the boiler installation and of its components, the manufacture of parts, and the erection on site of the boiler. The actual manufacturing operations involve general mechanical engineering and metallurgical technologies and the processes by which most parts are made, and some components themselves, are suitable for the manufacture of other products. This has led to considerable variation in the extent to which water-tube boiler suppliers themselves carry out the detailed operations required by their contracts. The supplier may himself manufacture a wide range of products some of which he may sell to other industries; on the other hand, he may manufacture only a small part or no part of the physical components of the boiler installation and may draw supplies from general mechanical engineers as well as from manufacturers of specialised components, who may include other water-tube boiler manufacturers; in any case, the water-tube boilermaker takes overall responsibility for the contract and the eventual product is his by virtue of design and his responsibility for construction and erection to the satisfaction of the customer.

18. The scope of the Association covers land water-tube boilers and all plant ancillary to such an installation. It may appear to have an arbitrary limit in that it excludes marine boilers. These latter, however, are generally on a much smaller scale, involve more repetition of design, etc., and the responsibility for manufacture and installation and dealing with the customer, as distinct from design, are often given to a distinct industry – shipbuilding. Water-tube boilers within the scope of the agreement all involve large-scale products and have a number of peculiarities in common.

19. A land water-tube boiler is different from the ordinary run of manufactured products. It may use a good deal of standard components – pipes, instruments, etc. – but the boiler is a very individual unit, tailored to suit the customer and the general operating conditions he lays down, to fit in with the generating plant he is installing or the general use of steam in the case of an industrial installation. Considerable variations in

specifications and operating characteristics have to be catered for. In particular, because of home conditions in our coalfields, the British industry has been used to designing plant to suit the available coals, which will vary greatly in quality and character from one site to the next, and to allow for the possibility of the considerable varieties of coal which may be delivered over the twenty years or more of the economic life of individual boilers.

In recent years, the need to use 'inferior' coal has accentuated this characteristic. Lord Citrine has characterised the fuel supplied to generating stations in this country as 'a quality of coal which is scarcely consumable in any other industry' (*Report* of the 26th Meeting of the National Joint Advisory Council of the Electricity Supply Board, 11 October 1957). It is worth noting the interest which the Russian delegation (whom I accompanied on part of their visit, see para. 5) took in members' achievements in fuel economy, and their particular interest in the extent to which our plants were designed to make use of a wide variety of different fuels. Their own practice was to design an installation for a particular fuel and tell the customer what it was; and the idea of having to design a boiler specially to take whatever fuel the customer had most easily available seemed quite foreign to them. It is, however, useful experience for export trade, where W.T.B.A. members have designed plants to use strange fuels – feathers, a local by-product of chicken farming, is one example mentioned to me – coal with a very high moisture content and varying ash content, and so on.

20. A boiler contract has to go through a number of stages, so that the construction of a large boiler will take years. There may first be preliminary calculations before any sort of final inquiry is made (this is particularly the case with the more advanced designs of plant where the customer may consult plant manufacturers informally at the planning stage). An inquiry will then be issued and a date given by which tenders have to be in. Once a tender has been accepted, instructions to proceed are given to the suppliers. The signing of the formal contract may not take place for some time – perhaps not until after the boiler is in commission – but manufacture and ordering of components, and so on, can start from the instructions to proceed. The stage of manufacture is followed by that of erection, which may for a large boiler be nearly as long again. Such a boiler cannot be made as a whole and then shipped to the site; the cost of assembly makes it impracticable even to erect it first in the shops for testing. It has to be put together for the first time on the site and this is a lengthy and skilled business. When the boiler comes into commission, the client will not officially take over responsibility for it

until he is satisfied on all details of the contract, and this may be immediately, or weeks, or many months, after commissioning. Quite apart from this, there is a twelve months' maintenance period from the date of commissioning during which the supplier is responsible for the replacement and putting into operation of any material which proves to be faulty.

It will be apparent, therefore, that there may be a number of circumstances lengthening the time of construction. For instance, there may be planning delays; permission to use a proposed site may not readily be given. Then the design of a boiler can greatly affect the time taken; the design itself may be subject to variation as a result of discussions with clients or later technical experience or information. National emergencies and capital investment controls are other factors which have operated in practice (see para. 45).

### Structure of the industry
21. The peculiarities of the product and its manufacture and sale have largely determined the structure of the industry. It is not a small-scale industry and no firm is small in any ordinarily accepted sense of the adjective – the annual boiler turnover of the smallest W.T.B.A. boilermaker is some £2 million. The relatively few businesses in the industry means that it is an oligopoly and any one firm by changing its price or other terms may enforce significant alterations in those of the others.
22. While all businesses involved are large, some specialise on boilermaking and some have boilermaking as only a part of their total activities. Their organisation varies greatly; on the one hand, firms are large enough to produce most components for themselves with reasonable economy of manufacture. On the other hand, they need not produce anything on the way to the completed boiler; they can buy all the equipment from other manufacturers, themselves performing the classical function of entrepreneurs, contractors and designers. It follows that there is a complementary as well as a competitive relationship between boilermaking businesses in this country. Some are specialist producers of components and may get lower costs and other commercial advantages which will be reflected in their prices for components, through the increased economies of scale attained by their doing work for other firms. Some of the largest specialist firms in the Association do considerable sub-contracting for non-members of the Association as well as for members. The special relationships between members seem however to be responsible for sub-contracting between members having been built up to a larger extent and some of it involves a greater exchange of technical information than would be freely given to outside competitors.

23. The following brief notes on members will show this variety of size and structure. The notes have been compiled from the current *Stock Exchange Year Book* supplemented by information from members themselves.

*Babcock and Wilcox Ltd.* Carries on the business of designers and builders of water-tube boilers, nuclear reactor-vessels, heat exchangers, cranes, etc. A large specialist firm with a number of subsidiaries in the country and subsidiaries or associated companies overseas including Germany and the United States of America. Issued capital £11,688,553; current assets £38,859,172. Eighty per cent of its activities by value are in water-tube boilers coming within the scope of the Association and in ancillary steam-boiler plant and equipment. The remaining 20 per cent is mainly in marine boilers and in other land boilers outside the scope.

*Clarke Chapman and Co. Ltd.* are substantial mechanical and electrical engineers, as well as boilermakers. Issued capital £1,509,850; current assets £4,272,737. About 55 per cent of their total activities are estimated to be represented by boilers within the scope of the Association and ancillary plant. The rest includes ships' deck and engine-room auxiliaries, mechanical-handling equipment, pumping machinery and lighting equipment.

*International Combustion Ltd.* Formed as a merger in 1934. A big specialist producer, 80 per cent of its activities being in water-tube boilers within the scope of the Association and the remaining 20 per cent in ancillary steam-boiler plant and equipment not associated with boiler plant. It does a considerable amount of sub-contracting and some of its products, e.g. milling equipment, pumps, centrifuges, have other uses besides water-tube boilers and are sold for general industrial purposes. It has a number of subsidiaries and overseas companies in Africa and Australia and maintains a close liaison with an American producer. Issued capital £3,027,735; current assets £12,325,467.

*John Thompson Ltd.* Originally John Thompson Engineering Co. Ltd, it still keeps its wide background but is now a holding company with 14 subsidiaries in this country and 7 overseas. As well as all types of boilers, its products include stokers and auxiliary equipment, heavy and light pressings, welded tanks, structural steelwork, metal windows and doors, water-softening plant, coal- and ash-handling plant and conveyors, heavy and light castings, steel gridway flooring, industrial instruments, etc. Issued capital £2,577,571; current assets £12,391,282. John Thompson Water-Tube Boilers Ltd is one subsidiary and is a non-manufacturing organisation, doing design and contracting only, but with many of its purchases coming from within its own group. Figures for water-tube boilers within the scope cannot be segregated from others, but all types of boilers taken together with ancillary plant and equipment are manufactured within the group and represent about 37—40 per cent of the group's activities.

*Simon-Carves Ltd.* A specialist design and contracting organisation with a number of subsidiaries at home and overseas. Originally they were not manufacturers at all and still, although some manufacture is done within the group of associated engineering companies, the majority of their requirements are made outside. A major product is coke ovens and the company also sells coals washers and chemical plant in addition to boilers. The latter, water-tube boilers within the scope and ancillary equipment, represent some 23 per cent of their total activities. Issued capital £1,500,000; current assets £10,586,824.

*Yarrow and Co. Ltd.* Engineers, shipbuilders with a considerable reputation as well as boilermakers; all at one works in Scotland. There is a subsidiary company in South Africa. The manufacture of water-tube boilers within the scope is about 35 per cent of their total activities. Issued capital £750,000; current assets £6,225,809.

24. There has been no accounting investigation of the members of the Association since, I understand, the Registrar agreed it would not be relevant. Moreover, it will be clear from the description of the activities of boilermaking businesses given above that it would not be easy to make precise accounting comparisons between businesses because of the important differences in their organisations. One obvious source of difference arises as between the two companies (Simon-Carves and John Thompson) who are contractors only, so far as their boiler divisions are concerned, and the firms who manufacture an important proportion of their components. Even among the latter, although the amount they actually make will vary a good deal, it is always true that a large part of a boiler is represented by work given out. Further difficulties arise in the separation of boiler work from other work; the large firm may keep its component departments fully occupied with boiler work; smaller firms especially will run the work in with similar products going to customers in other industries. In this way, the organisation of work keeps overall costs down to economic levels but part of the costs of the manufacture of boilers is necessarily entangled with the costs of producing other products.

25. A further accounting difficulty which arises but which is very relevant to the case is that of separating out overheads from other costs. A great deal even of the labour employed in the works and on erection must be considered as overhead rather than variable prime-cost labour, in so far as it contains a body of highly skilled men who are no less a part of the permanent organisation of the business than the higher-level staffs. Firms will not dismiss these in the short run even if the current volume of work does not fully justify their retention. Further, research and development cannot be separated entirely from the production costs, in so far as each large boiler installation has unique aspects; the two sides react on one another, research solving production and running problems, and the problems which come up in practice leading to advances in research work. This is one reason why ability to do this kind of work, with the substantial research organisation behind it, is essential to get big contracts, and may be explicitly required.

26. Despite these difficulties I should have liked to have had a survey conducted by skilled outside accountants, but in view of the limited time available, I sent a simple questionnaire to members who provided figures showing the make-up of their costs under broad subdivisions. It was stipulated that I should not disclose individual figures, so I have aggregated them and give percentage figures only in Table 3. The figures are for the four manufacturing members only. The position of the two firms who are contractors only really should be discussed separately in view of the peculiarity of their accounts, but it is not possible for me to do this since that would involve the effective disclosure of their individual information. Their figures naturally show a preponderance of overhead costs, works labour, for example, being reported as nil. The problems of allocation are such that the figures must be regarded as approximate in any case, but certain facts stand out clearly.

27. For these four manufacturers, sub-contracted material bought out (h) is the largest single item, being 43 per cent of the cost of work done. In contrast, the prime-cost materials on which further work is done in the shops (a), is a relatively small proportion. About 21 per cent, or nearly double the latter item, is made up of works, erection and other wages and salaries (b, c and d). The remaining costs, 15 per cent of the whole, are the costs of design and research staff, repairs etc. and depreciation costs (e, f and g). To estimate what costs are overheads, it would probably be conservative to take half of the wages and salaries figures (b, c and d) as fixed costs given the organisation of the businesses. Adding these to the costs of e, f and g, we get that something like one-quarter of all costs in these four firms taken together will not in the short run vary with output and must be incurred if the organisation is to continue.

28. Of these fixed overhead costs, only depreciation and obsolescence (g) do not involve the immediate paying out of cash. (g) is only 2.6 per cent, so that over one-fifth of total costs is 'paying-out' or cash overhead costs – which is quite a heavy proportion. If there is a fall in output or prices which means that these costs cannot be recovered from turnover, there is a drain on the cash resources of the business.

29. The weight of overheads and especially cash overheads in this industry means that at all times businesses have a strong inducement to run as fully as possible, so as to reduce the incidence of overhead costs per unit of output, and so improve their competitive position as much as possible. The timing of future contracts is uncertain and payments for work in hand will end at foreseeable dates. Contracts accepted will pass through the various departments of the organisation at uneven rates and will involve a varying amount of activity for the business. To take on more work with the right delivery date attached will mean that the balance and flow of work can be adjusted in the interests of economical working. Contracts for smaller industrial plants dovetail with central station work. Even when they are apparently full of work, boilermakers are therefore eager to get more if customers will accept any lengthening of delivery dates involved. For this reason businesses will not usually pass by a serious invitation to tender without quoting.

30. These considerations will mean that a firm whose order book is short and which is weak financially will be driven to take additional work to help fill its works at any price which will make some contribution to its financial burden. It will be reluctant to cut the overhead organisation which it needs for its long-term success but eventually it will have to cut research and design staffs and its nucleus of skilled labour.

31. The preponderance of overhead costs means that one cannot assume that the prices which will be quoted even by competitive firms in a completely free market will bear a close relation to their current costs. A very efficient business will ordinarily quote prices which are higher in relation to its costs than are the prices of its weaker rivals to theirs. But the price which any firm will quote for a particular contract will depend upon the value it attaches to getting that contract in the then-current circumstances. For this reason, even in times of high demand, a business which normally gets a high profit margin (has low costs, may quote a relatively low price for a contract which will serve as the basis for a medium-term expansion programme, or which will increase its general prestige or which will fit conveniently into its production programme. Similarly, a weak, high-cost business at times when it is short of work may quote for contracts at prices which show actual losses. In this industry it

cannot be assumed, as the Registrar does (ref. *Answer*, para 10(c) and (d)) that the 'distribution (of work) produced by conditions of free competition would be in the public interest' and that 'over-employment and under-employment . . . are . . . adjusted by differing efficiencies prices and delivery dates . . .' Where there are relatively few businesses, of differing financial strength with overheads an important part of total costs, and where orders are obtained competitively through infrequent contracts from large buyers, it does not follow that the firm who quotes lowest has the lowest costs for a given quality of product, or is using less of scarce productive resources available for other uses than is the case with those who quote higher prices. Businesses might well be driven from such an industry when their average costs were lower than some of the businesses who remained.

### Conditions of demand and the market

32. The demand for water-tube boilers is a derived demand – derived from the primary demand for electrical generating plant and steam-raising plant. When considering the responsiveness of total demand to changes in prices, we must distinguish between electrical generation and large-scale industrial users on the one hand, where there is no effective substitute for water-tube boilers, and on the other hand, relatively small waste-heat and industrial steam users for whom there are feasible alternative methods of raising steam. For the first, total demand will be inelastic, will not change much in response to changes in price; for the second class, reductions in water-tube boiler prices may push out the margin at which they will be used so that demand may increase, and increases in prices may reduce demand.

33. While total demand will therefore be unresponsive to price changes the demand for the products of an individual producer, if he should reduce his price against the price quoted by other producers, will of course be very elastic. (I am leaving on one side for the present the effect of monopsony – dominance in the market of individual buyers; this means that it is not necessarily true that a producer will get increased orders if he lowers his price. The fact that he has cut his price may be used to induce others to quote at even lower levels).

34. When referring to prices, the qualification should be read into all statements – 'given the quality'. Delivery dates may also be a factor in competition and when the industry is generally pressed, a producer who can offer an earlier delivery date may be able to get a higher price. In conditions when capacity is adequate, or more than adequate, for current demand, however, we may ignore this point because any producer to

obtain a contract must offer as early a delivery as his rivals, as well as being competitive on price. Subject to these points, it follows that in this industry a producer cannot sustain or improve his relative position unless he quotes prices which are no higher than his rivals and the stress of competition will tend to produce prices which on average work out at the same level as between producers. Meanwhile, in the shorter period, the elasticity of demand should ensure that price differences reflecting different views taken by producers of the desirability of particular contracts, operate to direct demand to the lowest bidder.

35. Lower costs of operations obviously give a boilermaker greater freedom of manoeuvre when deciding what prices he will quote for any particular contract. A boilermaker strives to simplify designs so that he may be in a position to offer the same effective quality of product at lower prices because his costs are lower. In the same way he tries to develop designs which offer his customers advantages of lower operating costs, e.g. through more easy maintenance, or greater reliability. Success of this kind of development of design will give him competitive advantages even at the same price as competitors until they have matched or adopted the new features.

36. While total demand will be very inelastic in response to price changes, it will be at least moderately elastic with respect to changes in national income. One element in the total consumption of power and process steam varies directly with the national income; another reflects the general trend towards substituting processes using more power for those which use less. Underdeveloped countries overseas may be expected to show even more steeply increasing demand for power in the long run than this country, for their use of power will rise directly with the pace of their development. One's view of the future movement of demand in this country and in overseas markets for the products made with the help of water-tube boilers is bound therefore to be an optimistic one. Recessions may bring a temporary halt but they cannot reverse the trend. The actual level of demand for water-tube boilers will be affected by the technical factors – the greater efficiency of generating stations and the move towards larger boilers which is a partial cause of this – which will have lowered the quantity of boilers required for given outputs of steam and electricity. But this trend cannot continue indefinitely without being overtaken at least for fairly long periods by the rising demand due to the trend of consumption and incomes. It will be seen therefore that present difficulties are temporary when measured on a reasonable time-scale. (Ref. para. 60.)

37. The point remains, however, that apart from any fall in the

general-level demand for water-tube boilers with income and activity because of the technical factors referred to above there will be periodic fluctuations in demand around the long-term trend because of fluctuations in incomes and activities. The demand for new water-tube boilers as distinct from replacements will vary with changes in income, etc., rather than with the level of income, so that industrial demand and overseas demand at least will tend to fall off sharply in periods of depression and rise equally sharply in times of boom. The demand coming from public authorities is open to influence of government policy on anticyclical investment. In recent inflations we have seen severe restrictions imposed on the generating industry's investment outlay.

38. Table 4 shows the demand coming to W.T.B.A. members in terms of orders. Over the five years 1954–8 on the average, of the total orders 47 per cent were work for the home central authority, 12 per cent were work for other customers at home, and 41 per cent were for overseas, whether for central stations or for industry. The table shows how in any one year there may be big fluctuations in the orders placed by any one category of customer but by reason of its size the changes in the volume of orders from the central authority dominate the overall picture.

39. In view of the fluctuations in home demand, members of the W.T.B.A. rightly attach great importance to maintaining their established position in the export markets and have tried hard to maintain exports even in times of peak home demand, subject to directives or requests from the Government. And as can be seen, total export contracts received by members are nearly as important as those taken from the central station authority at home. (The home activity resulting from foreign contracts is of course reduced by the value of work done abroad.) Table 5 shows the overseas trade position for territories within the scope of the agreement in more detail for the years 1954–8, and it will be seen what a dominant position W.T.B.A. members hold in those territories. The amount going to other U.K. producers is small by comparison and perhaps even more striking is the small proportion placed on average with our very strong competitors who include German and American makers.

40. Such a position is a good basis for further expansion when overseas demand resumes its normal progress. The territories include many underdeveloped countries and as their industrialisation proceeds there is likely to be a rising trend in the demand for our exports. But it should be noted that the position of U.K. manufacturers can only be held if they maintain competitive prices. There is a general tendency for the prices of heavy capital goods going for export to be very keen (excluding the abnormal post-war period of a seller's market); this does not necessarily

mean lower prices than at home, but the higher costs inseparable from export selling are likely to involve lower profitability. There are a relatively large number of international manufacturers competing for exports, and at any one time there will normally be one who is prepared to quote very low prices to get a particular contract (for the same reasons as described above, para. 31).

41. The smaller industrial orders which make up the bulk of the rest of home orders are important to the industry just because large orders come in large discontinuous lumps. For efficient production, and more especially with recent trends in home central station demand, even the large producer needs a proportion of these smaller orders to fill in the gaps and give him the continuity which efficient planning of production requires. But some industrial orders will in fact be sizeable in relation to individual firms' turnovers and in relation to the total work available at the time when the contract is offered.

42. This brings me to one permanent feature on the demand side which must be brought into consideration: the oligopsonistic strength of very many of the industry's customers because of the size and importance of their individual orders. The ignoring of this fact is a grave weakness in the Registrar's *Answer*. The powerful position of the C.E.G.B. and its predecessors is clear from Table 4 but the following figures, taken from statistics provided by the Registrar, show the average contract prices of boilers supplied by W.T.B.A. members to the C.E.G.B. on contracts with starting dates from 1951 to 1958.

| Year | No. of boilers | Average contract price per boiler (£000) |
|------|------|------|
| 1951 | 32 | 753 |
| 1952 | 37 | 705 |
| 1953 | 14 | 1,013 |
| 1954 | 3 | 1,622 |
| 1955 | 22 | 1,425 |
| 1956 | 4 | 2,250 |
| 1957 | 6 | 1,874 |
| 1958 | 6 | 2,793 |

I shall discuss in the next section of my evidence the extent to which the C.E.G.B. has actually exercised its market power and it will be appropriate later to consider how far that power might be exercised in conditions of completely independent competition on the suppliers' side.

43. In my opinion, however, much smaller buyers than the C.E.G.B. have in present and foreseeable circumstances sufficient buying power to be

able to influence prices and terms of particular contracts in their favour, granted the small number of contracts which make up total demand and the even smaller number which will be known to be available for competition at any one time. Table 6 shows the substantial size which has been attained by orders from non-C.E.G.B. customers, both home and overseas. It will be seen that there are quite a number of sizeable orders by any standpoint. But the really relevant standpoint is in relation to the individual firm: how many orders in any one year will be powerfully attractive to individual members, so that any customer with an order of such a size will have the power, in the absence of the agreement, to play one supplier against another.

I decided to measure the attractiveness of an order by comparing it with some definite proportion of the total market which was in fact enjoyed by each of the individual members in each of the years 1954–8. The definition which I decided to take was that an 'attractive' order is one which is more than 20 per cent of the orders currently received by an individual firm, setting these out firm by firm. I defined the denominator of my percentage to include all water-tube boilers within the scope of the Association, excluding nuclear installation orders. The orders whose sizes I considered did not of course include any C.E.G.B. and nuclear power station orders; and I assembled them into home and overseas orders separately. Table 7a, therefore, gives an indication of the potential attractiveness of home non-C.E.G.B. orders, and Table 7b gives this for all non-C.E.G.B. orders including overseas orders within the scope of the Association.

It will be seen that in any one year there are normally a very fair number of customers whose individual orders are attractive to at least two and even three members of the Association so that they could un-doubtedly 'play the market' as between at least those members. As a separate point: I know that members attach great importance to continuity of work with particular clients, and this factor in itself will increase the market power of particular individual purchasers of water-tube boilers, but I cannot take account of its effect, important though it is, in a statistical manner.

It will therefore be clear that an individual contract which is far smaller in relation to total annual demand than are the contracts and orders of the C.E.G.B. will nevertheless often be a large proportion of the new market demand which can be foreseen at the time when it is put out to tender. It is just because individual contracts in this industry have this power of attraction to members who will be wishing to assure the general balance of their order books, given the contracts which they have in hand, that individual customers whose aggregate demand is not large against normal annual totals of orders have in the past been able to employ the techniques of rebargaining (which the members refer to as 'Dutch auctioning') which the pure economic theorist tends to credit only to much larger buyers. (It will be realised that the market power of individual customers arises from the fewness both of buyers and sellers as well as from the sizes of orders.)

THE PRESENT CIRCUMSTANCES OF THE INDUSTRY
44. Before assessing the circumstances in which the Association's agreement has to be appraised, I examine recent history, and especially the growth in capacity of the industry in response to the post-war increase in demand. There has been a big increase in demand for electricity since the war. Total sales to consumers in England and Wales, which were 18,373 million units in 1938 were 32,669 million units in 1947–8 and consumption has risen every year since then to 72,661 million units in 1957–8. (Ref. Central Electricity *Report and Accounts*, 1957–8, Appendix 4.)
45. In the early post-war years consumption was held back by the shortage of generating plant which was a 'direct result of the war and the limitations on new plant construction then necessarily imposed by the Government'. (B.E.A. *Report and Accounts*, 1947–9, para. 140. All quotations in this paragraph are from the central authority's *Reports*.) It was the practice of the old Central Electricity Board to plan their commissioning programmes 5 years ahead (and successive authorities in the nationalised industry since 1948 have carried this on and extended the period more tentatively to 7 years ahead). The post-war programmes down to nationalisation, however, were hardly realistic. The first report of the nationalised industry makes it clear that these were based on an estimate of demand – 'the programme for any year consisted of new stations and extension to existing stations which, together with the reliable capacity of the existing plant, were considered to be the minimum necessary to meet the expected demand for electricity in that year.' (para. 149) The programmes which were established for the years up to and including 1952 were thus based purely on ideal requirements and 'called for a rate of installation more than double that achieved in any pre-war year'. (para. 150) I observe that this was at a time of inadequate supplies of labour and materials to the manufacturers, government controls on investment, etc. and government directions that exports should have priority.

Recognition that the manufacturers were hopelessly overloaded led to the authority's programmes for 1953 onwards being based on the capacity of new generating plant which could be made available. As a result, it was estimated that new plant would be brought into operation as follows:

| Calendar year | Capacity, (kW sent out) |
|---|---|
| 1952 | 1,150,000–1,400,000 |
| 1953 | 1,300,000–1,500,000 |
| 1954 | 1,400,000–1,600,000 |
| 1955 | 1,500,000–1,700,000 |
| 1956 | 1,600,000–1,800,000 |
| 1957 | 1,700,000–1,900,000 |

the lower amount being 'that which may be expected with confidence, and the higher amount that which may be possible if nothing untoward affects existing plans'. (1951–2, para. 45)

In fact the Government interfered directly with the programmes and set a limit on the annual amount of new generating plant of 1,550,000 kW (sent out) from 1955 onwards (1951–2, para. 47). Later this limit was raised for 1958 and 1959 to 1,750,000 kW (1952–3, para. 55), then altered to 1,950,000 for 1959 (1953–4, para. 95), and again altered to 1,650,000 for 1958 and 1,850,000 for 1959 (1955–6, para. 76).

The output capacity of new plant actually brought into commission in those years may be set against the programme (1957–8, para. 89):

| Calendar year | New generating plant (kW sent out) |
|---|---|
| 1952 | 1,492,000 |
| 1953 | 1,366,000 |
| 1954 | 1,375,000 |
| 1955 | 1,665,000 |
| 1956 | 1,797,000 |
| 1957 | 1,788,000 |

The drop in 1953 is explained in the 1953–4 *Report* as due to delays in power station construction: 'These delays were due to shortages of materials which resulted from the institution by the Government, following the outbreak of the Korean War in 1950, of a large defence programme to which the highest priority was necessarily given'. (para. 116) And the 1954–5 *Report* states: 'Although more new plant would have been brought into operation but for the shortage of materials referred to in the 1953–4 Report . . . the 1954 total, which was very close to the level of 1,450,000 kW sanctioned by the Government, reflected great credit on the manufacturers and contractors concerned.' (para. 84) Thereafter the plant position improves until the 1956 and 1957 additions which were each 'two-and-a-half times as great as the highest figure for any pre-war year and over five times as great as the total for 1947'. (1957–8, para. 90)

46. No direct figures for the boilermaking industry's capacity are available to put alongside the programme figures. But Table 8 gives the total annual output of members of the W.T.B.A. for the years 1952–6. This shows how the fluctuations in orders were necessarily smoothed out in actual production and how output grew steadily until its peak in 1955. The present capacity of members will be larger than the peak output figure of £60 million in 1955 because of the additions and improvements to plant, etc. which have been made since then. The 1955 output figure can therefore be taken as a minimal estimate of present annual capacity of members.

47. Even had there been no shortages of materials causing production difficulties, this is not an industry where it is easy to build up capacity quickly, since it is peculiarly a matter of building up the right body of men, in the design office (and a chronic shortage even of routine draughtsmen was a common complaint until very recent times), in the research department, in the works and for erection. When one looks at the achievements of the Authority and its plant suppliers, the disappointment at delays expressed in some of the *Reports* seems rather perfectionist. The general inflationary conditions affected all delivery dates, including those of suppliers on whom members of the Association had to depend. The mere statement that in 1952 the British Electricity Authority's programme 'required about ... 16 per cent of the structural and reinforcing steel available for all construction purposes ...'[10] calls attention to two of the practical difficulties in the face of which this expansion was made. Quite apart from the dependence on the availability of steel of the right sorts in the right quantities, the industry made heavy demands (and more than proportionately so for the boiler sections of the plants) on constructional labour which was one of the types of labour in shortest supply during the whole period of over-full employment. (For a general discussion of the effect of materials shortages, see B.E.A. *Report*, 1953–4, paras 116–118.) Other reasons outside the producers' control which extended the construction time for power stations were the bureaucratic system which held up approvals of schemes, duplication of work between divisions and headquarters of the central authority, and the tendency to insist on 'frills'. (Ref. *Herbert Committee Report*, (pp. 25 and 71: and Babcock and Wilcox's *Chairman's review* for the year ended 31 December 1946, where he refers to the need to try and standardise both coal quality and design:

If, however, regular supplies of graded fuel of known calorific value were available, and purchasers would be content during the next few years to accept types of steam-raising equipment of proved efficiency and design, much could be done to increase production. This is no time for frills and foibles – neither is it a time to allow the best to be the enemy of the good . . .)

The British Productivity Team which visited the U.S.A. found construction times to be much shorter there and were understandably keen to relate this to a criticism of the home situation – the alleged lack of competition between British manufacturers. But there is no evidence that I have seen that construction times compared so unfavourably with America before the war; and the C.E.A. *Report* for 1956–7 notes that the time taken to construct stations had been 'steadily reduced' in recent years (para. 118). An American team visiting this country in 1952, on the other hand, gave quite respectable reasons why our post-war performance should lag behind theirs in our post-war conditions. (For relevant extracts from the reports of both of these productivity teams, see the *Herbert Report*, p. 25.)

48. As an outside observer, from what I have seen of the industry, I am disposed to believe that most member firms did what they could to build up capacity again quickly. But, equally, I am not surprised that the electricity authority wanted capacity increased even more quickly in view of the national need for power. Whilst continuing to urge members to increase their capacity therefore, they tried to relieve the situation by encouraging additional businesses to make central station boilers. The *Report* for 1950–51 describes efforts 'to expedite the delivery of plant': 'In the case of boilers, for example, manufacturing arrangements have been made with a very large engineering concern which has not hitherto made land boilers of the type required for large modern power stations, and contracts for some of the smaller units have been placed with firms who have not in the past undertaken work for power stations to any large extent. As a result of these efforts, nine firms will be supplying the boilers which come into commission during the six years 1951–6, as compared with five for the corresponding period 1945–50'. (Para. 82 – the latter figure is not accurate, according to my information, but I deduce that at this date the authority had persuaded four new suppliers to come into the market.)

49. In so far as the intention behind this was the stated one of adding to the capacity of the industry, I may observe that adding new enterprises

could do little to overcome the effects of shortages of special kinds of labour and materials; indeed, further competition for them and their employment by yet more firms may very well, in the then prevalent circumstances, have made it more difficult to achieve the target outputs. But it is also clear from the later *Herbert Report* (p. 119) that the Authority thought that increased competition would lead to a reduction in prices. Apart from any perverse consequences of the kind referred to in the first sentence of this paragraph, it is relevant to this object of the authority that the Association was then operating its old agreement under which work flowing from competitive tenders was encouraged to go to the selected members, who for each contract and subject to certain limitations were enabled to set a price to be covered by the other members tendering for the contract.

50. It seems likely that there was some understanding between the electricity authority and the newcomers about the future volume of work which they could expect. (Ref. Lord Aberconway's speech at the annual general meeting of John Brown and Co. Ltd, 1958, quoted in para. 149 below.) Some such arrangements were made by the C.E.A. with C.A. Parsons and Co. Ltd after it had withdrawn, apparently at the C.E.A.'s initiative,[11] from the price arrangements covering large steam turbo-generating machinery in the home market in so far as the customer was the C.E.A. (though it still co-operated on prices to all other purchasers).

51. The British Electricity Authority early instituted 'discussions on price questions . . . with the chief manufacturing concerns. Two associations of manufacturers accepted the principle of independent investigation, by a mutually acceptable outside firm of accountants, of manufacturing costs incurred in typical contracts'. (*Report* 1950–51, para. 308). Lord Citrine in the speech quoted earlier (report of the *Proceedings of the Sixth Electrical Power Convention*, Eastbourne, 1954) went on: 'We feel that it is much better for the firms, through their associations and through special arrangements which will be made for this purpose, to give us reasonable assurance of what their costs are . . .'. The W.T.B.A. were among the first to co-operate in this way, and some arrangement was very nearly come to, I understand, but the attempt was abandoned by the authority. No explanation was given, but the abandonment coincided with the investigations of the Herbert Committee, and the stress which the C.E.A. put there on 'competitiveness'.

52. I wish to make it clear that I do not blame the electricity authority for exercising its power as an 'oligopsonist'. Indeed, since I do not find that completely free competition is economically desirable in this industry, I look to the beneficial operation of what has been called

'countervailing power' as between suppliers and purchasers, and think that the long-run safeguard is that the scales will if anything, be tipped rather in the favour of buyers. It nevertheless is a fact which is in my view relevant to these proceedings that the authority has exercised its power – and it has exercised it directly in its relations with W.T.B.A. members.

53. One instance of this may be referred to – that of the eleventh boiler for the Brunswick Wharf Power Station: the first ten boilers at this station had been built by Clarke Chapman and Co. Ltd and it was expected that they would receive the order for the eleventh boiler, but it was in fact given to John Brown's who had recently entered the field, despite the fact, as the W.T.B.A. believe, that they had submitted a quotation which failed to satisfy the consultant engineers and the B.E.A., both with regard to price and design. It is indeed clear that the B.E.A. did not wish John Brown and Co. to use their own design, for they pressed Clarke Chapman to supply Brown's with their design and full working drawings for the first ten boilers so that Brown's could build the eleventh to the same specification.

54. Statistics illustrate this general picture. Table 9 shows the pattern of contracts placed by the C.E.G.B. and its predecessors and how they have been 'allocated' by the authority or awarded 'competitively' between W.T.B.A. members and non-members respectively. The table shows how non-members have increased their share of the market through C.E.G.B. policy. It shows how temporary was the marked change in policy in 1955 – towards placing tenders competitively with all boilermakers – and in fact this policy was persisted in only for W.T.B.A. members. For the last three years any work which non-members obtained was allocated to them; the fall in their share of the market 1958 suggests they have not sustained their position even under these conditions. The following is a further illustration of the position:

*Percentage of Total MW Going to W.T.B.A. Members*

| Year | Of allocated contracts | Of competitive contracts |
|------|------------------------|--------------------------|
| 1951 | 76.6 | * |
| 1952 | 85.0 | 100.0 |
| 1953 | 87.2 | 64.3 |
| 1954 | 64.0 | * |
| 1955 | 94.3 | 47.7 |
| 1956 | nil | 100.0 |
| 1957 | 25.0 | 100.0 |
| 1958 | 18.2 | 100.0 |

*There were no competitive contracts at all with starting dates in these years.

55. Evidence from the C.E.G.B. may establish how far members and non-members are today getting orders competitively against each other either on technical achievements or on price. Statistics, however, suggest that W.T.B.A. members are not generally uncompetitive. The smaller non-members who were indeed induced to undertake work for the authority (ref. para. 47 above) seem to have left the market: Bennis and Adamson have had no contracts placed with them since 1951, and Richardsons Westgarth has had nothing since 1953. On the technical side, Table 2 has already shown that the average size of boiler placed with members over a period has been consistently larger than that produced by non-members. That table shows that the largest boilers at any one time are always produced first by a member and only later, when the broad technology has been established, are they made by others.

56. So far as price is concerned, the following figures have been derived from data provided by the Registrar and give the average price per megawatt of all W.T.B.A. boilers supplied under C.E.G.B. or earlier authority contracts as a comparison with the prices of non-members:

| Year | Average price of W.T.B.A. boilers per MW as percentage of non-members' boilers' average prices per MW |
|------|-------------------------------------------------------|
| 1951 | 89.6 |
| 1952 | 102.7 |
| 1953 | 105.8 |
| 1954 | 87.0 |
| 1955 | 109.7 |
| 1956 | 80.2 |
| 1957 | 100.4 |
| 1958 | 91.7 |

I regret that I am not capable of suggesting in what ways these averages should be modified to allow not only for differences in the average size of boiler but also for differences in novelty and difficulty of construction as between members' and non-members' boilers, but on the face of it, it would be difficult to assert that W.T.B.A. members have failed to achieve competitive prices as a general rule. In four out of the eight years W.T.B.A. members' prices have been substantially below those of non-members, the largest difference being 20 per cent in 1956; in the other four years, their prices have been comparable in two years and higher in two years, the largest difference being 10 per cent in 1955. It would have been interesting to make a direct comparison of the prices which both parties achieved in competitive tenders alone, where presumably techniques are most comparable, but the Registrar has not provided the data from which this can be calculated.

57. Against this background of the effects of C.E.G.B. policy must be placed the fact that in the last 18 months there has been a general falling off in the demand for water-tube boilers. A standstill in C.E.G.B. programmes coincided with a halt in the growth of industrial activity at home and an export recession. It is now becoming clear that the industry is over-expanded for the immediate future home demand. Chairmen's speeches all refer to growing excess of capacity. The chairman of John Thompson Ltd said in July 1958 that only three contracts had been placed so far that year for conventional boilers by the C.E.G.B.; and the chairman of International Combustion Ltd said that the C.E.G.B. did not issue any major inquiries until late in 1958. At the same time, with the increasing size of boilers, what central station work there is will be placed in fewer contracts. Individual contracts are substantial in relation to the capacities of individual suppliers and are generally of significant size in relation to the total capacity of all suppliers. The smallest maker in the Association recently obtained a contract worth £6½ million, whereas its annual boiler turnover was only £2 million. The High Marnham power station contracts of International Combustion involved a total sum of over £14 million.

58. As regards the middle-distance future, the C.E.G.B. commissioning programme is now understood to be as in Table 10 (the figures were announced at a meeting between personnel from the C.E.G.B. and plant contractors on 9 December 1958).

This table shows that contraction is planned until 1965. Thereafter an increase is planned, but the 1967 programme is still not so large as the 1961 one. The drop in the programmes of conventional sets is particularly marked and the trough year is 1966. Since nuclear work is outside the operation of Rule 5 of the Association, the position for this class of work is especially interesting. In effect, one may prophesy declining total activity on this account until 1962–3 at least, with fewer but larger boilers requiring decreasing work in total.

59. I understand that the Board, faced with this situation of over-capacity, are anxious that research by members shall continue, and that prices shall not be so driven down by competition as to endanger quality of plant or research, and that there should be some rationalisation of production. The situation has, however, quite largely arisen through the Board's own actions.

60. Looking further ahead, the situation does not justify pessimism. One would expect an increasing demand for electricity and that the trend towards ever larger steam boilers will level off. Apart from demand for

additional capacity, from about 1970 onwards there is likely to begin a big programme to replace some of the post-war boilers, since the economic life of a boiler is 20–30 years, and recent technical developments are likely to accelerate obsolescence. Further, present information does not suggest that nuclear power installations are gaining ground on the basis of overall costs, since conventional plant has shown itself capable of large and continuous increase of efficiency.

61. It would be a mistake, moreover, to concentrate too much on the lagging prospects for home central station demand. It would seem reasonable to forecast that other demands are likely to rise in the fairly near future. Home industrial investment is already beginning to pick up and has recently been further stimulated by Government action. Further, a probable revival in world trade will increase total demand there quite apart from the favourable effects of any increase in the rate of growth of relatively less developed areas of the world, which will have more than proportionate effects on their demand for energy. While exports may be expected to increase substantially in volume, they are likely to remain very competitive in price but increases in contracts both at home and abroad should fill the gap arising from falling central station requirements to some extent. It is in my view the next five to six years which are likely to prove the most difficult, with capacity remaining in excess of home demand to a large extent; but beyond that period the rising trend of demand should assert itself.

62. I submit that present and immediately foreseeable circumstances should be judged in the light of the desirability that the human and research capacity of leading boilermakers should not be run down more than is necessary, since a considerably greater capacity than that which is now employed will be wanted within the period which would be required to recruit and train the necessary design, research and control staffs, and in the light of the industry being able to get the maximum benefit from the export markets. The reasons why the working of the agreement in these circumstances should promote these objectives will be given in the following section of my evidence.

The working of the Agreement
63. I confine myself generally to the working of the present agreement, as operated by members of the Association in the present circumstances of the industry. It is however relevant to note that the previous agreement had two features which are not present in the agreement which is before the Court; I mention these because some of the economic assertions in the Registrar's *Answer*, although even then open to dispute, would appear to

have a more substantial basis in the earlier agreement than they have now.
64. The features of the former agreement to which I am referring are, firstly, that the chosen member fixed his own price, subject to objections from the other members interested in the contract who quoted an agreed amount higher; and, secondly, that this price advantage of the chosen member made for a loose system of allocation as between members.

65. Under the present agreement, interested members arrive at their prices independently, and a member who thinks that he may become the selected member for a particular contract and who wants to get it must try to quote the lowest price before the Association's tendering arrangements operate. If he fails in this, the most he can do, and then only if he succeeds in becoming the selected member, is to put in a price which the other interested members will accept as the equivalent of the lowest price otherwise tabled. There is, correspondingly, no artificial financial penalty in the way of the customer exercising a preference for a non-selected member. To me as an economist there appears to be a substantial difference between the principles on which the two agreements have been constructed.

66. The restrictions involved in the Agreement which I consider in this section of my evidence arise under Rule 5 which comes into play when more than one member gets an inquiry with regard to the same contract. Mr McKillop has explained the actual operation of Rule 5 in considerable detail in his Proof of Evidence and I should like to comment on the working of Rule 5 in the light of the statistical analysis before the Court.

67. The statistics show that, from the date of the present agreement until the end of December 1958, 1048 inquiries were notified to the Director; 688 of these were sole inquiries where the customer chose to approach only one member of the Association, so that its tendering arrangements were inoperative. I am concerned with the remaining 360 inquiries and at first sight I myself considered the number of these where Rule 5 was actually operated – 83 – to be disproportionately small, having regard to the benefits which the Association claims to follow from the working of its agreement. A study of the matter, however, showed that these 83 inquiries are much more important in relation to the actual business available for competitive tender since the inception of the agreement, than their mere number might indicate.

68. As the statistics from the Association show, 28 must be deducted from the 360 because it would be misleading to include them in relation to the 83 – these 28 cases are 17 which were inquiries discussed immediately after the signing of the new agreement and before the procedure had had time to operate, and 11 are inquiries which were notified to the director

before 31 December 1958 but had simply not then been dealt with. Mr McKillop has further explained the relatively small groups of cases where the procedure could not be operated, or it was agreed it should not be operated, or it was operated under local overseas arrangements which have since been terminated. Eliminating all these leaves 197 cases, of which the larger group consists of the 113 inquiries where the operation of Rule 5 was deferred. These inquiries frequently involved members being asked for preliminary or budgeting quotations. I consider it reasonable that the operation of Rule 5 should be deferred in such cases; for one thing, members will be quoting on the basis of inadequate data compared with that available when the precise specifications have been decided; for another, to deal with the matter under Rule 5 in connection with such preliminary quotations, at what may very well turn out to have been a very early date, could lead to difficulties in view of the stipulation that members may not vary prices when they have been tabled except as allowed by Rule 5, the whole tendering arrangements being designed to ensure that only serious, and not provisional, prices are put on the table.

It would, I think, be quite misleading to classify these 113 cases as ones where Rule 5 has not been operated. In fact, a number of them involve only very tentative proposals and come to nothing within any reasonable period after the inquiry, but the main reason for my unwillingness to classify them simply as Rule-5-not-operated will appear if it is assumed that all of them do become firm inquiries and so are later dealt with under Rule 5: supposing that no other inquiries are involved and that these themselves are put only once as preliminary inquiries and once as firm inquiries, then the statistics might apparently show that Rule 5 operated in only 50 per cent of cases, although it would really have governed 100 per cent of all the contracts concerned. In so far as some inquiries may be raised more than once before a firm tender is invited, the proportion of Rule 5 cases on such a classification might well appear to be appreciably below 50 per cent.

69.  Leaving aside the one case where Rule 5 was operated up to the point at which members discovered that they could not agree on a selected member, the importance of the remaining 83 cases where the tendering arrangements under Rule 5 were in full operation may be indicated more directly — by trying to estimate the total value of the contracts involved in the inquiries. The total value of such contracts may be put at approximately £51½ million,[12] which makes it clear that a substantial proportion of members' trade has been governed by the operation of Rule 5 since the coming of the new agreement.

70.  I now turn to the economic effects of this agreement. I confined

myself to trade conditions which now exist or which I think can reasonably be foreseen. In particular, I shall assume that it is unlikely that war or immediate post-war conditions will return — the conditions where a heavy excess of demand became a normal affair. (If we were to see the return of such conditions, I think there are grounds for arguing that the net effect of the present restrictions would be to cause prices to be appreciably lower than they would be in completely independent competition.)

71. I may also note that, in reaching my opinion, on the effects of the present agreement, I have been influenced by the signs that I have seen that there is keen competition between members of the Association, and by the view which I have formed that members of the Association have made a genuine effort to work an agreement which has none of the price-fixing or allocation features of the old agreement.

72. I shall first analyse how the existing industry would behave without the Association's agreement, with all present members competing quite independently. The industry has relatively few customers and I shall assume that all buyers will try to buy on the best commercial terms open to them. This assumption covers the C.E.G.B. who have been publicly advised by the Herbert Committee to be guided purely by commercial considerations and not by any notional idea of the national interest. (Ref. *Report*, paras 28, 372, 373 and 507; the C.E.G.B. 'should have one duty and one duty alone: to supply electricity . . . at the lowest possible expenditure of resources . . . ' etc.) I have already referred to the position of smaller buyers (para. 43) and shown that a considerable proportion of their orders are sufficiently large for them to have the power of beating down suppliers, and I here assume that they would exercise it — indeed since they come relatively infequently to the market they are likely to be more indifferent to any long-term consequences of their actions: and there seems no especial reason why foreign buyers should think it necessary to have great regard to adverse consequences for the British industry.

73. In addition to the assumption in paragraph 70, the assumptions which I make about market circumstances in this industry are broadly that (i) central station demand at home will remain relatively low for some years, with relatively fewer and larger contracts making up the demand which does arise, (ii) industrial and overseas demand, both on the low side at present, will soon begin to revive, (iii) in the longer term, the trend of world incomes and activity should continue to rise and the trend of the demand for energy and power, and with it for water-tube boiler installations, should rise even more sharply owing to the continuing tendency to substitute mechanical energy for human power — so that the

longer view must embrace a need for increasing productive capacity rather
than less.

74. How would prices behave in the near future in this industry if the
suppliers were in completely independent competition? Without putting
definite figures to one's prophecies, it is possible to say that there would be
a heavy downward pressure on prices so long as total capacity were larger
than demand. This pressure would come partly from the competition of
suppliers for what business is going but its effects would perhaps be
especially marked in certain sections of the market. Central station work,
the basis of the trade, would be especially attractive and the larger
businesses would compete particularly strenuously for such work. Because
of the limited home market, competition for any sizeable export orders
would inevitably lead to low prices there. In all sectors, the effect of
oligopsony, of the market power of relatively few buyers, would be to
depress prices still further.

75. As shown in paragraph 31, in these circumstances there is no rational
short-period floor to prices. The extent to which a firm will cut prices and
yet stay in business will depend upon its other resources and upon factors
which have nothing to do with current costs of production. There will be
no resistance to the pressure on prices so long as sufficient businesses are
so short of work that additional work seems attractive at the prices which
can be got.

76. The consequence of such price conditions must be a corresponding
pressure upon the maintenance of the overhead establishment which I have
already shown a water-tube boiler business needs to maintain. I shall argue
later that the Association's collective research would have collapsed with
the demise of the agreement, but now the long-term 'unproductive'
research undertaken by a business itself would have to be cut. When a firm
is anxious for business, accurate estimates are not important and a cut in
estimating staffs may well appear possible. In bad trade conditions there
may be serious inconvenience to customers through businesses working
with minimum staffs, avoiding overtime, etc., or even just abandoning
contracts unfinished, in order to minimise the losses arising from their
faulty estimating. After that will come a cut in design staffs, and then in
the technical day-to-day research activities – in anything in fact which the
business can do without in the immediate short run. But in my view this
industry has not permanently redundant resources and it would take a long
time to replace the staffs, etc. which will be required again when demand
once more catches up with capacity, which might be assumed to have
become seriously shrunken if conditions of unrestricted competition had
been allowed to prevail for some time.

77. I should further make the point that if independent competition will drive resources from the industry which it is reasonable to expect will be required in the foreseeable future, it does not follow that the work which continued to be available would be distributed between firms so as to make the best use of available resources. The firms which would be driven from the industry – those with more profitable branches, or those with less resources currently available in cash form – will not necessarily be those who are least efficient or those whose displaced real resources can be most economically used elsewhere. Historical experience suggests one consequence – the concentration of production in fewer units – which does not seem desirable in this industry. This is not the case of a mass-production industry where there may be economies of concentration; what production economies there are can be obtained through sub-contracting. On the other hand, in this industry, there is clearly advantage in having a fairly large number of units of planning, research, design and production in order to provide the most favourable long-term conditions for development and growth.

78. I think it may now be helpful if I state the ways in which the present agreement may cause the members to behave differently as compared with what would happen if they competed in absolute independence. The reference is, of course to those contracts which have been put to competitive tender and where interested members have agreed to operate Rule 5 and choose a selected member.

(i) Members who are interested in the contracts affected by Rule 5 normally inform each other of the prices they intend to quote – at the table after the selected member has been determined – before they tender (though if any of these members has for one reason or another already submitted his tender, which is of course permissible, such member if he asks for and receives the 'selection' may not be able to exercise his right as the selected member to reduce to a lower price because his submitted tender is unalterable).

(ii) A selected member, if he has not himself tabled the lowest price, is permitted to go as far to meet it as he chooses in his offer on the main scheme, with proportionate reductions (but no more) for alternative schemes if he so chooses.

(iii) The prices to be quoted by all members are settled by them at a date which is slightly earlier than the tender date, and which may be earlier or later than the date at which they would individually have settled their prices in unrestricted competition.

(iv) No member may subsequently vary the price he quotes for the boiler-plant installation as put out to tender or for any alternative scheme he submits at that time. (I am for the most part ignoring the possibility of some agreed latitude under Rule 5(h) but see para. 129.)

(v) In cases where the selected member did not independently table the lowest price and exercised his right to come down to it, the customer will have the choice of one extra supplier at that lowest price.

79. The circumstances in paragraph 78 follow directly from the terms of the agreement. It will be convenient here to list also other present circumstances of the Association which seem to me to be unlikely to occur in a competitive industry:

(vi) The maintenance of a record of trading of the kind kept by the Association.

(vii) The preference given to other members in the matter of sub-contract work.

(viii) The maintenance of collective research.

80. I shall now discuss one by one the effects of the circumstances referred to in paragraphs 78 and 79. I shall review their general overall effect later, but it will be seen that they do not prevent the working of competition in the way I have described in the present conditions of the industry but rather tend to moderate the excessiveness of its consequences.

81. In independent competition (see (i) above), a firm will be guessing blindly at the level of price at which it would have the chance of a contract. It can infer the movement of prices only by what it can learn of the prices at which previous contracts have been awarded. Whilst it is true that businesses may be misled by their own levels of cost and tend to quote too high for a contract which they are anxious to get, this will correct itself – or over-correct itself – with experience; and the general result is that businesses in the worst situation panic and quote lower prices than they need. In this way the general level of quotations for later contracts will be unnecessarily forced down. Any customer can make this situation worse by playing on the supplier's fears and hinting at lower prices being obtainable from others.

82. The tabling of prices under the Association clearly prevents the kind of oligopsonistic manipulations of the market to which I have just referred. A sure knowledge of the trend of competitive prices will even help the supplier facing a customer on an 'allocated' negotiated contract. As Mr Brown's evidence show, the continuous tabling of prices is a great advantage to the smaller firms but it probably enables all members to make better predictions of what will be a realistically low price.

The extent to which a member cuts his price will still be affected by the urgency of his need for a particular contract. His success in the contract itself, where there are outside competitors, as distinct from success at the table of the Association, depends on his price being low in relation to the prices quoted by outsiders. Since, however, the Association includes some of the largest and probably lowest-cost firms in the industry, who are likely to be particularly embarrassed by shortage of work, the clue to a realistic price policy given under the Association is probably as effective *vis-à-vis* outsiders as it is *vis-à-vis* members.

In this way I find nothing in the arrangements of the Association which makes for rigidity of prices but rather would expect what I understand to be a fact — that the pressure of competition within and without the Association has caused prices in recent years to fall relatively to costs; and I know that members of the Association expect that this will continue in the near future even under the present agreement. What the arrangements achieve is to moderate the fall in prices more nearly to that which is justified by the underlying real situation in the industry and in the individual firms.

83. The right of a selected member (see (ii)) to reduce his tabled price: the selected member may, of course, decide that he cannot afford to reduce his price all the way to the lowest evaluated price tabled, that he does not want the contract so badly as to reduce the profit available from the contract so much as the maximum possible reduction would entail, or that, having regard to other factors — such as the technical features he offers — he need not in fact reduce by so much in order to get the customer to look at his offer equally favourably. The fact that he is offering an 'alternative scheme' may be important here. A selected member is permitted to make the same proportionate reduction on an alternative scheme as on the main tender.

It is of the essence of alternative schemes, however, that they involve technical inventiveness to offer the customer something more economical than he has thought of, or to meet his requirements more attractively in some other way. Alternative schemes are not evaluated and only bare technical details are tabled with their prices, so that valuable information is not directly revealed before the innovator has had a chance to get an actual contract. Nevertheless, the knowledge that something involving technical innovation has been done will stimulate other members.

84. The tendering arrangements do not form an allocation system in the usual sense that the customer is presented with an artificial penalty for choosing other than the selected member. The supplier who tabled the lowest price will remain in that position of advantage, compared with others except the selected member, when the tenders go in. If the selected

member makes the full reduction open to him, the member who originally tabled the lowest price will now face the competition of an equally attractive offer; and, as I have said, the customer will have the choice of two tenders at the lowest price tabled.

85. Apart from the direct effect of the arrangements, explained in paragraph 84, there is the question of what indirect effects are implied in the foreseeable circumstances. I earlier concluded that the general effect of the arrangements in such conditions was that prices would not be driven so low under the Association as they would be in blind, independent competition. That conclusion refers to the general level of prices; there remains the question of relative prices as between members on any one contract. A business which has no current basis of claim for selection or is doubtful of success with such a claim will in any case, if it wants the contract, have to try to table the lowest price; and the assumed conditions mean that for any sizeable contracts most businesses will want to be in the running. The principal question, therefore, is how far a member who may hope to be selected will 'pull his punch' and table a higher price than he would have quoted had he been competing independently.

86. It is relevant to recall the grounds on which a member can claim selection: (1) preference of customer for his designs as a result of long and close connections, (2) a clear position of vantage in a local market, (3) a relative shortage of work in hand, (4) a need for the contract in order to get experience of new technology at an early stage, (5) (probably) the existence of heavy local unemployment around his works.

(1) and (2) are indeed circumstances which will enable a firm to get a higher price than others without its advantages. But it will have to have regard to the levels of competitive prices and it seems misleading to concentrate on the possibility of the firm 'pulling its punch' because it may later be able to revise its price to meet simply the competition from within the Association. (3) and (4) are circumstances which might well make him anxious to obtain the contract even at a lower price than any other member would be prepared to quote. The possibility of easy expansion of some of his operations implied in (5) might in other conditions of trade conceivably make him willing to go lower in his prices, but I do not think it necessary to pay much attention to this as a ground for selection in present circumstances.

87. Where a selected member has a customer attachment, he may not need to set so low a price as others in order to obtain any one contract. But he may nevertheless, for long-term reasons, not want to have other members tendering at lower prices than himself — and I am convinced that this weighs with the members of the Association with whom I have

discussed the matter. There seems to be a strong desire to avoid the position of being generally 'out on price'. Where he has no especial advantage with the customer, it will be clear that if he really wants a contract he must try to go into tender at the lowest price and will not wish to be only on level terms with a competitor. In present circumstances, moreover, it will be very rare, especially for home orders, for a member to feel confident that his co-members will agree to his being the selected member for any particular contract. The claim to a buyer's preference will probably have to be much more convincingly proved in conditions of general deficiency of demand, if other members think that they would have a chance of the contract on equal or better prices than his. Such a claim is then very likely to be disputed by those who feel themselves to be worse off, and to persist in it could easily cause the breakdown of the Association arrangements. In general, then, it seems to me that a member who has only this basis for his claim, if he really wants a particular contract, will be likely to decide that the only safe thing to do is to try to table the lowest price and not rely on the outcome of the discussions.

88. It would appear that a member might have greater confidence in a claim which was based on relative shortage of work; he will know the general record of trading of other members in recent periods. There would seem, moreover, to be likely to be less opposition to such a claim in so far as, if they grant it, the other members are assured that if he succeeds in the actual contract they will move up in the queue for selection.

At the same time, it does not follow that the member in question will necessarily succeed in, or persist in his claim to a particular contract; so that there will be some uncertainty about his chance of selection. To be most short of work on the record of trading does not mean that one is in the most stringent financial position and a member may well have to recognise some urgency in the plight of another. Equally, as already said, a member who is in such a stringent situation may well table a low price, and a selected member may well decide that, since his position is not so desperate, he does not wish to reduce down to or near that level.

89. There is clearly much uncertainty about the position of a member who wishes to claim selection on the ground that he would like experience of newer technology. The relatively large contract for the home central station authority for which his claim would have to succeed will be very attractive, and may even appear vitally necessary to, the larger businesses who have already helped develop the technology. It is equally likely that, because of its cost position and lack of experience of carrying out such a large contract, it will tend to fix on too high a price as being low for such a contract; to that extent such a business needs to succeed in its claim and

use the privilege of a selected member to be able to reduce its price to a level which will not penalise it. In so far as this is the case, selection on this ground cannot be related to higher prices to the customer at all, but must simply be taken as implying a widening of his choice at the lowest price quoted by those with experience of such contracts.

90. My general conclusion, therefore, is that the arrangements for selection do not prevent the quoting of competitive prices to the customer by any of the members. This conclusion is reinforced when account is taken of the fact that a claim for selection succeeds only as against other members; for his chance of getting a contract to succeed, the member tendering the lowest price, whether as selected member or otherwise, must quote a price which is competitive with outsiders' prices. In presently foreseeable circumstances in this industry I find no reason to doubt the general truth of members' claims that, before coming to the table, they quote a keen competitive price according to their current circumstances and that the selection arrangements are simply designed to enable selected members to improve their relative chances in the contracts for which they have been selected, if they should happen not to have tabled the lowest price.

91. I turn to paragraph 78 (iii) – the settling of prices at a date which is somewhat earlier than the tender date. Since the meeting is held as near as possible to the tender date, this is a very trivial matter and I do not propose to discuss it further, especially since any slight effect which it might have will be of the same class as that entailed by the fourth feature of the tendering arrangements which I discuss in the following paragraphs.

92. I now consider (iv) – that no member may subsequently reduce his price for the contract in question, or for any alternative scheme which he submits with it.

93. If between the date of tender and the date of awarding the contract there is a major change, e.g. a reduction in prices of materials, the customer will expect a repricing. What the agreement does prevent is that a member, having learned the prices of other members, should then lower his own price to the customer to a level which would get him the contract. For him to exploit his knowledge in this way would rapidly lead to the breakdown of the Association; but it seems to me that I need not discuss this any further because nothing analogous could occur in independent competition except in two circumstances: first through improper disclosure by an employee of a manufacturer or of his customer, and second, a customer's intentional disclosure of price for the purpose of beating down his contractors. I disregard the first; the second is a serious possibility, but if it were a regular practice, contractors would tend to put up their tender

prices in order to be able to reduce them later. The regulation in itself therefore tends to ensure that prices quoted under tenders are realistic ones and not intended to allow for haggling of a kind inimical to the working of an effective contract system.

94. I observe that there is nothing in the agreement which prevents a buyer from altering the design of his plant so as to lower its cost and then reoffering it so as to get a competitively lower price from fresh tenders. Neither does it prevent a buyer once he has awarded a contract, or announced an intention to do so, from discussing with the supplier ways and means of altering the specifications so as to get the price down, still with the possibility of reoffering the amended contract if he is not satisfied with the reductions in price offered by the originally chosen supplier.

95. The widening of the choice of the customer by the inclusion of the selected member (78(v)), states its own direct effect briefly. There is the important question of how far the necessity to reduce his price, if the selected member has not already tabled the lowest price, will have any effect on the quality of the installation. Such an effect seems to me to be alleged, by implication, in the Registrar's *Answer*. The motive which may be assumed for such conduct is, I suppose, to recoup himself for the lower profitability of the contract if he gets it at the lower price.

96. I find it difficult to believe that one particular kind of reduction of quality could occur – where a member would cheat on the design and construction of his plant so as to lower the quality of what he had contracted to deliver according to the customs of the industry and his own practice. Virtual fraud of this kind would anyway seem to be ruled out by the expertise of buyers or their advisory engineers.

97. It may be suggested that the selected member who has reduced his price would reduce the specifications in his tender as it actually goes to the buyer, so that he would offer an explicitly lower-quality job, or at all events a cheaper job, than he originally proposed to offer at the price he tabled. The following considerations seem to tell against this:

(i) This would be against the rules of the Association, but, quite apart from this, the process of evaluation of tabled prices means that a member whose price is higher *only* by reason of greater operating efficiency or more expensive components, etc. will not be out on price.

(ii) This is a tendering industry with a high proportion of fixed costs and the price for any one contract will not be determined in any precise fashion by the exact accounting cost of executing it, which will depend very largely upon the total activity of the supplier during the period when he is carrying out the contract and so will be known only at a much later date.

(iii) The meeting under Rule 5 takes place so near to the tender date that the details of design will have been determined, and to alter them would involve the supplier in considerable expense as well as exposing him to risks because of the last-minute changes in design details.

(iv) The great majority of buyers being experts, or buying on expert advice, a supplier may expect to get a contract at a higher price which really is consonant with higher quality except in circumstances of extreme depression on the buyers' side – in which case any overriding interest in low monetary prices would seem likely to have already determined the specifications of the plant.

98. I call attention again to paragraph 94.

99. It might also be suggested that quality of work might be affected even if the tender goes in as already planned but if the selected member, on getting the contract, applies pressure on his suppliers; and it may be thought possible that they will achieve lower prices only at a cost of a reduction in normal standards of qualtity in their work.

Supposing that such a reduction in quality of sub-contract work occurred with the consent of the main contractor, the considerations I have already mentioned arise and it is difficult to see that it would be in his interest to accept the situation. It is even more difficult to see that they could occur without his knowledge or early discovery (and much sub-contract work is for standard or semi-standard equipment). So that the sub-contractor would soon endanger his own goodwill – with the clients, moreover, as well as with his immediate customer.

100. This is not to deny that a selected member, like any other offerer of work under contract, may ask his sub-contractors to requote for a particular contract. Both parties would understand, however, that usual standards of quality would be required. What does seem unlikely is that such recontracting could be a regular feature. If a member did make anything like a regular practice of this, his sub-contractors would soon 'allow something for a reduction' in their quotations, which would be against his direct interest since he would then lack a firm guide to his own price quotations.

101. I may finally note that the necessity to ask sub-contractors to re-quote for a job is much more likely to occur in unrestric ed competition where customers are exercising their oligopsonistic powers. In fact the arrangements of the Association make the practice less likely than it would be otherwise. (I observe that if there be anything in the idea that this

practice reduces the effective quality of work then it would follow that this detriment to the customer would be substantially more prevalent in unrestricted competition.)

102. Leaving the deviations from competitive conditions which are involved in the actual working of the tendering arrangements, I turn now to the other circumstances which I listed in paragraph 79 as unlikely to be found in unrestricted competition.

First, (79(vi)), the maintenance of a record of trading of individual suppliers: this could conceivably occur in a completely independent competitive industry but I think it extremely unlikely that information of this kind would be compiled and circulated. Regarding its effects, I have already explained that such a record will yield general information about current trading conditions and about the fortunes of individual competitors which would tend to mitigate some of the extreme competition which will occur when general trade conditions are very adverse from the suppliers' point of view, where the worst-hit firms will otherwise tend to assume that others are as desperate as they are. This has therefore a conceivable sustaining effect on the general level of prices quoted in such conditions.

103. Second, (vii), the preference given to other members in the matter of sub-contract work: this encourages a more even spreading of the work arising from contracts, thus helping to prevent or mitigate any tendency towards drastic short-run cutting of prices in periods of excess capacity. I shall refer to this in more detail later, as also to the longer-run effects through the wider development of such sub-contract work, which will tend to lower the normal level of costs and therefore of prices.

104. Lastly, (viii), the maintenance of collective research: the effects of this have been described in Mr Simonson's evidence, and I summarise them as tending to produce better or cheaper boilers. Although collective research is not impossible in conditions of unrestricted competition I think that effective research of this kind would be abandoned if the agreements were to go, but discuss this opinion later.

105. In what follows I shall now consider the benefits and detriments, in the light of the Restrictive Trade Practices Act, which appear to follow from my conclusions about the probable effects of the agreement. I indicate the benefits which I think arise from the tendering arrangements as a whole, of which the restriction that members may not subsequently alter their tabled prices is an essential element. The benefits will first be stated in general terms and then I shall try to relate them to the specific provisions of Section 21 of the Act.

106. As is normal in economic analysis, I shall assume that the term

'benefit' covers the avoidance of a detriment which would occur if the agreement did not operate, as well as the securing of a benefit which is a positive result of the working of the agreement.

107. Unlike many restrictive agreements, the Association's tendering arrangements do not prevent short-term flexibility of price to meet significant changes in the relationship between capacity and demand. Because prices will therefore reflect the underlying real circumstances of the industry there seems to me to be nothing in the Association's arrangements which will tend to maintain excess resources in the long run. If a firm cannot match the prices sustained by the most efficient member it will have to go out. What the arrangements do tend to prevent is what I have called panic prices which not only will be unjustified having regard to the actual situation concerning the balance between demand and supply capacity but may even worsen the long-run position from the point of view of customers and of ordinary consumers farther down the line.

108. I think it is a benefit resulting from the arrangements that productive capacity and capacity for research and development will be kept in being to a greater extent than would happen if the members were in completely independent competition in presently foreseeable circumstances.

109. The phrase 'to a greater extent . . .' is used because competition within the Association's arrangements does cause prices and profitability to fall in circumstances like the present. It follows that there are already some pressures towards the reductions of firms' capacities. In my opinion, however, present circumstances, if unrestricted competition prevailed between members, would cause a much more drastic lowering of prices and this in the longer run would entail a reduction of capacity which would be detrimental to purchasers, from the point of view of the efficient meeting of home demand in the foreseeable future, and to our competitive position in the export markets.

110. Not merely would capacity be unnecessarily reduced; short-run excessive competition of the kind I envisage would also probably have the effect of favouring quite unnecessary amalgamations between businesses — unnecessary from the longer-run point of view. I have already argued that a reduction in long-term efficiency would probably result from the reduction in the number of independent centres of design and development.

111. It is to be remarked that in so far as capacity fell short of eventual demand it could be enlarged quickly only at substantially higher costs. (It seems to me that post-war experience has some relevance here.) Prices would therefore tend to be higher than if the agreement continued to operate.

112. It is relevant here that each of the member firms, at some point or other in its history, has made an original contribution to design and the subsequent exploitation of that feature must have led to a valuable variety of technical viewpoints on matters of detail. The number of competitors is small already; it does not seem in the public interest, having regard to the importance of continued technical development, that it should be reduced further by the elimination of members of the Association whose continued existence is commercially justified in the light of the more favourable market circumstances which can be foreseen.

113. I have already indicated that in my view the efficiency of members of the Association is substantially increased in present conditions by reason of the encouragement given to the placing of sub-contracts as between members in preference to buying outside while members have the necessary capacity available. The effects of any reduction in contract work as a whole are thus mitigated by the curtailment of outside sub-contracts so that members' establishments work more nearly to capacity and therefore more efficiently. In this way the Association has available a flexibility of output which helps to preserve members' general efficiency, and (if, against all reasonable expectation, the present lack of demand should be greatly prolonged) to prevent any wasteful locking up of resources. Not only will all firms in such conditions carry a greater proportion of work previously given outside, but one or more of them may become mainly or entirely engaged on sub-contract work – when they would still be sub-contractors who can draw on their previous intimate knowledge and experience of the industry. I know that the possibility of being far more dependent on sub-contract work has been taken into account in the capital investment decisions of at least one member. As before, it should not be overlooked that any business kept in more efficient being in this way will still be available as a separate unit of enterprise whenever demand later justifies the renewed expansion of the industry.

114. I do not see the partial displacement of outside sub-contractors as the source of any serious public detriment from the point of view of consumers and the general public, since members have such clear advantages as sub-contractors; further, the kinds of mechanical engineering and other techniques which the outside sub-contractors employ are in general quite capable of employment in the production of other kinds of goods without great loss of efficiency.

115. Members do, of course, act as sub-contractors to non-members, and this leads to the obvious point that the advantage which members can offer from their efficiency and experience and the gain to them of the

more full utilisation of their resources both make it likely that such sub-contracting would continue even if the agreement were discontinued. But it is my opinion that it would be less in magnitude than if the agreement goes on. Members of the Association have an increased feeling of public responsibility because of their agreement and certainly desire to avoid the dominant customer having any genuine ground for complaint that members 'gang up' in this way against outside competitors; I consider that this leads to a greater willingness to carry out sub-contracts for such people than would exist if the agreement disappeared. There therefore seems to me to be at least a minor benefit of the agreement here, that members make a contribution to the efficiency of non-members through being willing to undertake sub-contracts for them on a more extensive scale.

116. Granted the fewness of businesses in the water-tube boiler industry, the position of the smaller businesses seems to me to be of especial importance since technical developments and other factors have caused such a marked increase in the size of typical central station contracts, and one may expect some such trend to show itself in industrial contracts as well. The smaller business will be especially likely to benefit from the increased possibility of sub-contracting for other firms which I have argued is brought about by the agreement. I wish to call attention to other features of the tendering arrangements which have similarly favourable effects on the survival and competitive efficiency of smaller businesses.

117. One feature which has been mentioned earlier is the greater and prompter knowledge of the movement of prices which such a business gets because of the tabling of prices for competitive contracts. The benefit is, however, not only that it can more easily decide what prices to quote, although I attach importance to this; the tabled prices over a period of time also give the smaller business a valuable scoreboard on which to measure its own commercial efficiency and performance. In my experience one of the handicaps from which a smaller business suffers in its competition with larger rivals, especially in industries where the total number of businesses is small and the interfirm variation in size is great, is that it cannot maintain some of the continuous internal checks on efficiency which its larger competitors can sustain. This kind of information therefore gives such businesses a regular external stimulus to re-examine their own productive and commercial arrangements.

118. The growth of smaller members shows that the Association's tendering arrangements have not prevented them from achieving a greatly increased scale of operations during a period when technical developments in particular have required this kind of trend. In these conditions,

however, the future of the smaller business depends upon its ability to get early experience of new techniques which must typically be embodied in contracts of a size as yet beyond its usual experience. To have a chance to win such a contract, the business must ordinarily not be out on price (on the other hand if it can meet this requirement, it may very well get the contract because of the interest which a really large buyer has in checking the potential market power of the largest suppliers). The smaller business might very well be able to achieve costs which are sufficiently comparable with those of its larger competitors for it to be worth taking the contract at a price which would interest them, but by the nature of the case it is doubtful if it can make a good estimate of what costs are in fact likely to be when it is carrying out such a contract and placing sub-contracts on the scale which is involved. In completely independent competition, therefore, it might well quote too high a price for the kind of contract which I am discussing and so miss a rare chance of getting the required experience – 'rare' because it must get in while such installations are still at least in the in-between stage of development if it is to be able to compete when they become regular run-of-the-mill jobs. This is where the possibility of claiming to be the selected member can be very important. If such a claim is accepted, the tendering arrangements give him the chance, if he thinks he can possibly make a go at that level, of quoting at the lowest level of price as between members. Relations between members, moreover, will enable him to be sure of getting any necessary technical help with such a contract, even to the extent of drawing on 'know-how' which would not normally be given in a competitive field.

119. As an example of this regulation working to the advantage of smaller members I think that, after inquiry from members, I can cite the awarding of the Blyth home central station contract to the smallest business, Yarrow's. This had further beneficial effects so far as Yarrow's were concerned, because I understand that when they were negotiating the large Rooiwal contract in South Africa the fact that they had obtained the Blyth contract was one of the factors taken into account by the customer.

120. I turn now to the general question of the effects on research and the development of technical knowledge. General technical development in this industry has been and is proceeding at such a pace that research and its early application is of great importance. In fact, the increased efficiency of water-tube boiler plants and their greater 'availability' – which have been the consequences of improved technical knowledge following research – have been one of the major causes of the reduction in home central station demand which now faces the industry. I have already indicated that if there were no agreement the resulting pressure on prices

would be bound to impinge especially heavily on the staffs and other resources available for research and technical development. Impressive though it is that it may take three years to build a large boiler, it is also important not to lose sight of the fact that it takes up to 20 years to train a responsible research worker or member of a design team. For its kind of industry, the available information suggests that the members of the Association are indeed spending relatively heavy sums on their individual research and development organisations — as is consistent with their own view of the matter and the claims which they make for their achievements.

121. Next there is the question of the collective research — the research for which the Association as such is responsible, both under its own auspices and in collaboration with other bodies. Members' confidence in each other and the feeling of public responsibility which the fact of their agreement has created have I think been very largely responsible for making this possible. It is true that non-members have been admitted to some of the committees concerned and that this has taken place at the instance of the C.E.G.B. or its predecessors. But the record makes it clear that the Association has been the seminal influence here. Had there not been collective commercial arrangements in the industry there would probably not have been collective research arrangements in which outsiders could participate; and without the feeling of responsibility to which I have referred, there seems no reason to expect that members would have consented to such outsider participation in schemes where they bore the greater share of the financial burden.

122. I have already raised the important question how far one can expect collective research to flourish on any important scale where there are no agreed limitations on the ferocity of competition. I think it is true to say that wherever there has been collective research between competing businesses involving subjects which are very near to everyday commercial application there will be found to be a background of an agreement which is restrictive in some sense or other which is within the purview of the Restrictive Trade Practices Act. (Which is most definitely not to say that such research will be found in the case of every such agreement.) I have no doubt at all that this is so in industries where the larger firms carrying on effective research activities on their own account make up so large a proportion of the market as is the case in this industry. In independent competition such businesses see only too clearly the advantages of going their own way. In my view therefore, as I have said, collective research would not continue if the restriction went and the agreement collapsed.

123. I recognise that the C.E.G.B. has its own skilled technical staffs (although the *Herbert Report*, para. 67, implies a serious scarcity of these

a few years ago) and am aware of the high regard in which the Board is held in the world electrical industries. There is no doubt that the Board itself plays an important part in the industry's research and might take on further responsibility (although here again the discussion of its research activities in its successive *Reports* suggests that it has already a very considerable operation in hand, and I know that research activity is not a line where one can prophesy increasing returns to size whatever the existing scale). It is, however, an open question whether so large an enterprise would gain by taking on the manufacturers' part and doing even more of this kind of work than it has to do at present. There would also probably be some disadvantage through the increased concentration of research initiative in a single body. Quite apart from the C.E.G.B., however, there is also the rest of the market to consider: as far as the smaller home customers and overseas customers are concerned, it seems to me quite clear that the curtailment of the manufacturers' own design, research and application facilities would be a serious matter in that it would lower their long-run competitive powers in these markets.

124. I now turn to the question of the benefits which the tendering arrangements bring in the export markets. Table 5 shows not only the predominant part which members play in the total exports of the industry but also the large share which they have in the total water-tube boiler contracts known to the Association to have been awarded in territories falling within the scope of the agreement. It is also relevant to a later section of my evidence to note that exports contribute a substantial share of the total activity of members – and indeed that their exports are a substantial part of the total activity of the whole British boilermaking industry.

125. In my opinion the agreement contributes significantly to the maintenance of this export position; and members would not have so strong a position if they competed in complete independence; certainly they would not achieve exports of the same value. Before justifying this opinion in detail there are one or two preliminary points to be put forward. First, export trade is likely to be intensely competitive because of the keen and unrestricted competition between major producers of several nations. Second, continued success cannot be expected from casual competition directed at particular contracts only. A strong position calls for a good reputation at home (and members' success in competition for home station contracts plays a part here), and for considerable continuing expenditure in the foreign market on local sales arrangements and organisation. The eventual result is a fund of goodwill which can be relied upon, provided that prices are not out of line with equally well placed

foreign competitors, and provided that the reputation for quality is also sustained.

Third, reasons already given make it understandable that a member may have a stronger connection in some overseas markets than in others, and that if it has to close down its operations there it does not follow that another British company will get the orders it would otherwise have obtained; the competitor with the greatest chance otherwise might well be a German firm. Fourth, in the foreseeable circumstances, British water-tube boilermakers have every incentive to go for exports in order to fill the gap left by the fall in home central station demand. But in normal times, businesses with long-run experience of this industry, and organised on the substantial scale which applies to members, will seek to have some regular footing in the export markets to insure against the vicissitudes of home demand (including fluctuations imposed by policies of home authorities and governments) and to balance the load on their facilities arising from the construction of the very large home boiler units.

126 It will be clear from my analysis of the general working of the agreement that I am of the opinion that it keeps the export potential of members at a higher level in present circumstances than completely independent competition would do. The prevention of individual members suffering from absolute shortage of work, the keeping in being of capacity which might otherwise be needlessly driven out, the help given to members to acquire new technical experience, the maintenance of high standards of quality and of levels of research – these mean that more firms will be in a position to undertake exports and that leaders can remain leaders in the very competitive international market.

127. A continued presence and effort in the international arena is extremely important. The high capacities of members may make exports desirable to them, but the market will not be available at all easily without continued effort and expense whatever the fluctuations in the export market itself. The avoidance of excessive reduction of home market prices through panic price cutting means that financial resources are available for this purpose. A price-cutting war at home would reduce export potentials eventually. It would also and more quickly reduce export prices and so lower the balance of trade benefits from members' overseas activities. More subtly, perhaps, if the C.E.G.B. did not pay a proper price for the development of the new technology it needs, this would also reduce the export potential, because there will be a reduction in members' technical capabilities or, to the extent to which members retain their research effort, they will have less resources for other purposes, including the maintenance of their long-run position in the export markets.

128. The tendering arrangements recognise the position which individual firms will have built up in some particular export markets. If a firm can convince its colleagues that it is in the best position to get a contract, it will become the selected member.

129. Because of the importance of exports commercially and from a national point of view, the export side of the agreement is administered with greater flexibility than the home side. Overseas competitors are not bound by the agreement to stick to whatever prices they quote in their tenders and orders might well be lost by rigid adherence of members to this rule. If a member can convince his colleagues that he should further reduce his tabled price to get the order against foreign competitors then such a reduction will be allowed. But the restriction prevents a further and unnecessary reduction of prices simply because of internecine competition between members. Sometimes, however, the rule is not operated at all and is left 'free for all'.

130. It appears to me that some support to export prices is given by the fact that at present overseas customers, it is believed, accept the Association's arrangements as a matter of fact and know that members' prices are not open to a process of reduction by bargaining against them individually. If the arrangements are not allowed to operate in the home market, I consider that the changed relationships between members would make it very difficult for them to continue a purely export agreement. There is further the psychological effect on foreign customers of an adverse decision in the present case.

131. I now turn to consider the effects of the agreement *vis-à-vis* the market power and policy of the dominant buyer, the Central Electricity Generating Board, leaving aside the general effects of the power which other buyers may have in individual contracts. Having said earlier that I accept that members' export chances are dependent to some extent on their position in the home market as well as upon their continued sales efforts overseas, it seems reasonable to remark that in so far as the dominant buyer has gone out of its way to introduce new firms to the industry it may be presumed to have weakened the foreign position of members, and especially the larger members against whom I think its policies have had especial effect. I refer later (para. 149) to a speech of Lord Aberconway's which shows how unattractive the export markets look to such a firm; meanwhile members have been artificially debarred from some contracts which would have maintained or increased their prestige abroad.

132. The market for water-tube boilers is clearly not the kind of market which economists should analyse in terms of perfect competition. Even

without the fact of the agreement, individual firms are important parts of the whole on the supply side and there are few of them; even more is the demand side of the industry dominated by a single customer both by size of total orders and because its contracts are of special importance to individual suppliers.

133. This industry therefore presents a good case of the difficulty of predicting the level of prices at any point of time which exists wherever oligopoly faces oligopsony. In the absence of the agreement prices would move according to the shifting strengths of the parties. In foreseeable circumstances, the pressure on prices would be downwards and even if the C.E.G.B. were convinced of the adverse consequences of pushing its policy of buying cheaply too far (which may well be the case) it is difficult to see how it would know just when to stop exerting its commercial pressure and adopt what in the short view might very well appear as a generous price policy. In these circumstances, I am of the opinion that the agreement prevents the C.E.G.B. from acting to the grave deteriment both of the industry (since the terms on which it trades would be unfair) and of the public (in view of the general consequences) by reason of home prices being forced to too low a level.

134. The restriction that members shall not alter their tabled prices after the meeting concerned with a contract, prevents rebargaining with a dangled contract which is the chief source of detriment in present circumstances. (I do not, it will be noticed, assume that a public authority would further strengthen its position by false information about tendered prices; but this strategy must not be ruled out in the case of other buyers whose buying power I have treated as part of the general economic circumstances of the industry.)

135. This restriction is the minimum necessary restriction if members are to table prices which they have decided on competitively. There is, however, an important freedom which I have not so far mentioned – important because it ensures that the tendering arrangements shall not artificially reduce the number of tenders which a buyer shall receive: If a member receives an inquiry late, or is late with his estimating, so that in good faith he misses the meeting where prices are tabled, he may nevertheless tender direct. He does not have the information tabled at the meeting which discusses the tender and he is at liberty to put in what price he likes even if it should turn out to be below the price put in by the selected member. In other words, he acts as an outsider for this particular contract.

136. So far as the C.E.G.G. is concerned, I have already made plain my view that in foreseeable circumstances it has not only the advantages of

the market power which it exercises alongside the agreement but also the assurance that members compete keenly for such contracts as it places by competitive tender; this must affect favourably for it the level of prices which they quote. The agreement prevents the authority from being able to go too far so that its prices and terms are unduly low.

137. I now consider the benefits which I think members may claim to follow from their agreement in present and foreseeable circumstances and in terms of the Restrictive Trade Practices Act. I first consider the possible claims under Section 21 (i)(*b*), and summarise the provisions of that sub-section which are relevant:

> . . . that the removal of the restriction would deny to the public as purchasers, consumers or users of any goods . . . specific and substantial benefits or advantages enjoyed or likely to be enjoyed by them as such . . .

I think that the benefits I adduce are substantial in themselves and also, as will emerge later, when put into the balance against such detriments as also result from the restriction in the given circumstances.

138. The benefits which seem to me to be relevant to this sub-section are:

(i) The maintenance of production and design capacity of members at a level likely to be needed by the market accessible to them, at home or overseas, in the foreseeable future (paras 108, 109, 113, 114, 115 in particular).

(ii) The maintenance of members' important research and development expenditures and of the collective research undertaken by them (paras 120, 121, 122, 123, 126 in particular).

(iii) The avoidance of the necessity of a further reduction in the number of competing businesses and the encouragement of the growth and increased efficiency of smaller businesses (paras 110, 112, 116, 117, 118, 119 in particular).

139. It can be argued that these benefits are good in themselves even when looked at from the point of view of society (the sum total of the consumers of *any* goods) as a whole; they also all imply that prices of water-tube boilers and therefore the cost of steam and electrical generation will be lower in the future than if the agreement were abandoned and the industry reverted to completely independent competition. They all also imply the greater availability of water-tube boiler plant and (i) and (ii) imply that quality standards will be maintained and improved. All of them have favourable implications for the export trade, which is of course the especial concern of another sub-section.

140. In view of the probable detrimental effects of the unrestrained exercise of their market power by a considerable proportion of buyers, I add

(iv) The prevention of such detrimental effects. I include in this the effects of the market power of the C.E.G.B., which is more particularly relevant to the Association's claims under Section 21 (i)(*d*).

141. I am not sure of the precise economic distinctions to be drawn between the two parts of Section 21 (i)(*d*), to which I now wish to turn: but it seems to me that the second part is relevant to this case:

> ... that the restriction is reasonably necessary to enable the persons party to the agreement to negotiate fair terms for the supply of goods to any person not party to the agreement ... who, either alone or in combination with any other such person, controls a predominant part of the market for such goods.

142. It seems to me that any judgment of what are fair terms must take into account what in the absence of the agreement would be unfair to the manufacturer (e.g. the unnecessary loss of his business position) as well as any unfairness to customers or to the public generally.

I consider that the C.E.G.B. in the proper exercise of its commercial power would, in the absence of the agreement, tend to get unfair terms from members, in this sense that in the long run they would prove detrimental to the interests of manufacturers and customers at home and abroad, as well as of the C.E.G.B. itself. As examples of the extent to which the C.E.G.B. has used its power I cite the encouragement of competitors even to the extent of getting a member to supply designs, etc. to a new rival and the privileged awarding of 'allocated' contracts to non-members in recent years so that in present circumstances the market available to members has been unnecessarily, and may have been unfairly, reduced. (The favouring of outside competitors by directed contracts has occurred despite a declared policy of putting tenders out to competition.) I have already indicated that I do not know how the C.E.G.B. would draw the line between fair and unfair conduct, if it were to achieve the best commercial terms, as it has been exhorted to do by the Herbert Committee, and if it had the opportunity, at present denied to it by the agreement, of rebargaining on a contract once put out to tender.

With this background the benefits which may be claimed to follow from the increased strength of members of the Association by reason of the agreement are broadly those which I have already stated in paragraph 138. It is relevant to emphasise that nothing in the agreement prevents the C.E.G.B. from exercising its market power in general fashion – e.g. the exercise of a preference against leading members of the Association or the award of directed contracts previously referred to; nor is the competition of members to get such contracts in any way diminished so as to involve what appears to me to be a detriment. As part of the result of an arrangement which prevents bargaining on contracts in an unfair manner, the C.E.G.B. is assured of receiving the tender which would otherwise have come to it at the lowest level of price, or of receiving one or more additional tenders at that price.

143. I have thought about the matter and can see no injury to the C.E.G.B. by reason of the fact that it does not know which member has reduced his price, if any, and by how much it has been reduced.

144. The remaining sub-section of the Act to be considered is Section 21 (i)(*f*):

> ... that, having regard to the conditions actually obtaining or reasonably foreseen at the time of the application, the removal of the restriction would be likely to cause a reduction in the volume or earnings of the export business which is substantial ... in relation to the whole business (including export business) of the said ... industry.

145. Table 5, in my opinion shows that the export business is a very substantial proportion of the whole business of the members, and the large proportion which it is of total trade in export areas within the scope of the agreement. When considering the effects on the export trade of any abandonment of the agreement, it is also relevant that a significant proportion of export orders are individually large enough for the buyers to have the kind of power to influence individual contract prices referred to in paragraph 43.

146. In my view the cessation of the agreement in present circumstances would cause a serious reduction in the earnings from export trade. The facts to which I have already called attention imply that, without the agreement, there would be less resources for foreign competition but that the struggle for exports would be as keen as it is now at least. The effects of that competition would, however, be sharpened by unnecessary competition as between members and the exploitation of market power on the part of individual buyers. Because of the importance of the export trade to members I do not anticipate that there would, for some time at least, be any great reduction in its physical volume, but the total demand for water-tube boilers in the territories affected by the agreement being inelastic to changes in price, it follows from my expectation concerning prices that the total value of earnings would fall drastically. In the longer run, a continued reduction in the profitability of exports, taken into

account with the effects which may be foreseen of unrestricted competition at home, might well result in the volume of exports declining; exporting could well be much more difficult if members lacked the overall resources with which to maintain their overseas organisations.

In the foreseen circumstances, they will have to make savings where they can, and the maintenance of overseas organisation is akin to long-range investment. The consequences of any reduction of resources here will be insidious rather than short term. Similarly, research will suffer – and I note the Registrar's admission (*Answer*, para 11) of the 'vital importance' of technical ability and research background in the competition for exports.

147. The 'tailpiece clause' of Section 21 involves a balancing between the circumstances which may be considered to have been proved under Section 21 (i)(b)(f) or (d),

> ... and any detriment to the public or to persons not parties to the agreement (being purchasers, consumers or users of goods produced or sold by such parties, or persons engaged or seeking to become engaged in the trade or business of selling such goods or of producing or selling similar goods). . . .

I shall state what I consider to have been detriments arising from the restriction and from the tendering arrangements of which it is a part, and to whom the detriment arises. I shall also consider in general terms the detriments alleged in the Registrar's *Answer*.

148. The first possible detriment I take into consideration is that prices, for reasons I have given above, may be higher, but I do not consider that they will be unreasonably higher – without the agreement I consider that prices would be unreasonably low so that a detriment to the public, as defined in the clause of the Act, would follow. Long run, therefore, there is no detriment of higher prices on the average; the C.E.G.B., however, may well be paying relatively higher prices than it would if it could freely exercise its market power against individual members of the Association in isolation. And other, possibly less scrupulous buyers might also benefit unfairly from unrestricted competition. Apart from this factor, however, I conclude that prices under present circumstances will roughly be what would be reached in conditions of independent competition.

149. On the reasonableness of present prices, I am, as I have shown, impressed by the slightness of the obstacles which the agreement places in the way of members' competition with each other, and with the signs which I have seen of their competitiveness. I am also impressed with the extent to which there is important outside competition: this has to some

considerable extent not come into the industry spontaneously because of high profits, but been induced by promises and representations made by the C.E.G.B. or its predecessors. How the industry, and the competitiveness of prices under the agreement, look to such an outside competitor appears from Lord Aberconway's speech to the shareholders of John Brown and Company Ltd (quoted from the *Financial Times*, 8 September 1958):

> The Whitecrook works of John Brown Land Boilers Ltd have continued in full production, but the future of this business must be viewed with anxiety. Overseas competition is intense and prices unremunerative. At home the programme officially announced for the provision of electrical generating capacity by way of big nuclear stations has lessened the requirements for new thermal plant; while the rapid increase in recent years in the size of individual thermal units has severely limited the number of boilers that will be needed every year. The resultant load is quite inadequate to keep even a bare majority of the established manufacturers reasonably employed. The fact therefore has to be faced that there may be a considerable gap in steam generating work available to the Company from 1960 onwards, and this is receiving careful attention. It is pertinent in this connection to recall that the Company started in this business at the instance of the Authority.

150. There remain the various detriments specifically pleaded by the Registrar in his *Answer*, and it will be convenient to consider these in summary fashion here. The Registrar alleges in substance that free competition would produce a desirable distribution of activity and resources as between firms, would produce prices which are fair and reasoanble, and that the agreement gives an incentive to the selected member to reduce quality.

151. It is a defect of the Registrar's *Answer* that he dismisses the question of the market power of the C.E.G.B. and the S.S.E.B. with a statement that they are public authorities and so would not attempt to impose unfair terms. This pays no attention to the insistence of the Herbert Committee that the central authority should place no limitations on its commercial freedom and should not attempt to decide where the public interest lies. Nor does the Registrar consider how the exercise of its market power is to result in fair prices. The Registrar's assertions suffer also from non-recognition of the part the authority has played in creating the present circumstances and the fact that it has not so far awarded all contracts so as to ensure the maximum competition. To the extent to which the Board is,

overall, bound to show favour to any businesses it induced to enter the industry in more prosperous times, the effects of present shortages of demand will be unfairly concentrated upon members of the Association.
152. As regards the distribution of resources, the Registrar's *Answer* does not recognise that long-run economic factors would be irrelevant to the determination of prices if there were completely free competition between suppliers in this industry in foreseeable circumstances. One can be sure that unrestricted competition would direct contracts towards a member who was desperately short of work only when he had quoted prices born of his desperation. It is not in my view desirable to ignore the consequence on the whole level of prices of this competition, and the consequences for long-term efficiency of that level of prices.
153. As regards quality, I have already argued the point and concluded that I cannot see how the Association's tendering arrangements can have a deleterious effect on quality.
154. The industry has, in my opinion, genuinely tried to manage with the minimum restrictions consistent with the purpose of the agreement. Given the present and foreseeable circumstances I consider the public detriment arising from the tendering arrangements to be minimal; and I also take the view that unrestricted competition would be likely to mean not the fair exercise of competition but rather its abuse, with a resulting negation of the benefits which are usually assumed to come from industries where there is free competition on both sides of the market and where all entities are so small that they cannot affect their market situation by their individual actions and policies. Some of the Registrar's points are more valid with regard to such a theoretical state of affairs than they seem to be in the actual circumstances of this industry.

APPENDIX 4.1
General statistical note
There are two general sources (other than published material) for the statistics I have used in my evidence: (i) information from the W.T.B.A. or from its individual members, (ii) information collected by the Registrar.

*Information from the W.T.B.A.*
The W.T.B.A. assembles information primarily on orders placed with its members. This is the basis of Table 4. The figures differ from those in the 'record of trading' before the Court. The latter is a current running score: as soon as it is known that a member's tender has been accepted, the sum will be credited to that member; if, when the work is put in hand the contract is revised, as may well happen, the addition or subtraction from

the original tender value is entered in the year in which it is decided. The statistics assembled by the Association, however, give the value, as at present known, of the original contract, referred to the year in which it was reported.

As regards overseas orders, Table 6 was compiled by me from Association statistics. Table 5 was compiled by the Association after (I am told) getting special information from members. Tables 7a and 7b have been compiled by me from special returns made at my request by individual members. In the case of overseas orders, in some cases it has not been possible to include the full contract value but only an f.o.b. value; this is the case sometimes where members have subsidiary companies overseas who undertake the delivery and erection. To the extent that this is so, the figures tend to under-estimate the number of orders above a given size.

Table 8 was again compiled from special returns made by members. It was undertaken, so I was told, in response to a suggestion from the Registrar, that the Association's statistics, being on an 'order' basis, represented only 'expectations' and not actual production. Table 8 gives an estimate of work actually done during each year for 1952 to 1956; the figures for overseas business include all overseas territories and are on an f.o.b. basis.

The figures in paragraph 69 are from a schedule of values for the 83 inquiries, prepared at my request by the Association.

*Information from the Registrar*
The Registrar, in response to the Association's request for further and better particulars of some statements in his *Answer*, produced a summary of water-tube boiler contracts placed with W.T.B.A. members by the central authority 1951–8, and two schedules, one for members of the W.T.B.A. and one for non-members. The schedule for members gave, year by year 1951 to 1958, information for each contract placed by the C.E.G.B. under the following headings: Date of instructions to proceed; date of contract letter; contractor; whether allocated or competitive; station; boiler number; size in MW; price £. The schedule for non-members gave the same information for contracts placed with them, except that the final column of price was not given.

The schedule for non-members has been used without further question. The schedule for members was checked through by officers of the Association, and a number of differences with their records were found. At a meeting with the Registrar's officer most of these were resolved. There were three cases, however, where the Registrar and the Association could not agree on the year for which a contract was to be entered. In these cases I have followed the Association's opinion:

*Castle Donington, Boiler No. 1* was not included in the Registrar's list on the grounds that the member concerned had sufficient information to proceed with the contract before 1951. The member says that they did not have sufficient information to proceed until March 1951, and this boiler is therefore included in the 1951 figures;

*Blyth 'A', Boiler No. 1.* The Registrar maintained that sufficient details were available to the member to enable them to proceed in 1952, but the member says insufficient detail was available until 1954, so this boiler is included in 1954;

*Rugeley 'A' Boilers Nos. 1 and 2.* The Registrar included these in 1956 on the grounds that the specification was not agreed till then, but the date of commencement of contract in the contract letter is given as November 1955 and it is therefore included as a 1955 contract.

As a separate point: Boiler No. 4 for Blyth 'A' has been included as an allocated contract. A competitive inquiry was issued for boilers 2 and 3. Boiler No. 4, while strictly an allocated contract, was based on the price of boilers 2 and 3 and awarded to the same firm on the same date as them. The Association, while recognising the classification of the Registrar as formally correct, would contend that this contract was placed on a competitive basis.

There were also two minor disagreements on values between the Association's and the Registrar's figures. The only instance to affect the figures is Thorpe Marsh, Boiler No. 1, 1958, which has been included at £5,881,977 where the Registrar's figure is £5,914,110.

In order to minimise unnecessary multiplication of figures, I have used the Registrar's data, subject to the corrections stated above, rather than Association records, in Table 2, in paragraph 42, in paragraph 54, in paragraph 56 and in Table 9.

It will be observed that the Registrar's information did not directly give the value of non-members' contracts. These have been inferred and are used in paragraph 56. The method of calculation was as follows. The summary sheet provided by the Registrar gives the total values of contracts placed with W.T.B.A. members, and the percentage which this is of the total annual value of all contracts placed. We can therefore deduce the value of contracts going to non-members as follows:

| | Total value of contracts placed with W.T.B.A. members ($\pounds$) | Percentage of total annual value | Total value of contracts placed with non-members ($\pounds$, approx.) |
|---|---|---|---|
| 1951 | 24,390,136 | 74.8 | $24{,}390{,}136 \times \dfrac{25.2}{74.8} = 8{,}217{,}000$ |
| 1952 | 27,634,603 | 86.7 | $27{,}634{,}603 \times \dfrac{13.3}{86.7} = 4{,}239{,}000$ |
| 1953 | 12,377,923 | 80.0 | $12{,}377{,}923 \times \dfrac{20.0}{80.0} = 3{,}094{,}500$ |
| 1954 | 3,315,439 | 51.3 | $3{,}315{,}439 \times \dfrac{48.7}{51.3} = 3{,}147{,}400$ |
| 1955 | 28,017,433 | 60.5 | $28{,}017{,}433 \times \dfrac{39.5}{60.5} = 18{,}292{,}400$ |
| 1956 | 12,338,613 | 61.1 | $12{,}338{,}613 \times \dfrac{38.9}{61.1} = 7{,}855{,}500$ |
| 1957 | 11,244,687 | 55.1 | $11{,}244{,}687 \times \dfrac{44.9}{55.1} = 9{,}163{,}100$ |
| 1958 | 16,790,419 | 71.3 | $16{,}790{,}419 \times \dfrac{28.7}{71.3} = 6{,}758{,}600$ |

The figures given for W.T.B.A. members in this summary sheet were subsequently revised by the Registrar and so have not been used except as the basis, in conjunction with the percentage figures, of the estimates of the value of non-members' contracts.

Table 4 uses Association statistics assembled at the request of their solicitors in order to show the relative importance of the main classes of orders. The first column may be divided as follows so as to show 'conventional' and nuclear station work separately. The C.E.G.B./S.S.E.B. orders have been kept on the Association's basis to be comparable to the other columns of Table 4, but the figures on the basis used elsewhere in my Proof, viz. as agreed with the Registrar subject to the exceptions listed above, are noted for comparative purposes: (see p. 108).

Table 10: The report of the meeting referred to, notes that the figures in this table should be increased by approximately 10 per cent to allow for plant likely to be required for the South of Scotland Electricity Board.

Orders placed with W.T.B.A. members

| | C.E.G.B. and S.S.E.B. orders* (£'000) | Percentage of total orders | Nuclear power station orders† (£'000) | Percentage of total orders |
|---|---|---|---|---|
| 1954 | 3,363 | 12.28 | 1,953 | 7.13 |
| 1955 | 29,999 | 50.27 | 6,394 | 10.71 |
| 1956 | 8,812 | 25.64 | nil | – |
| 1957 | 11,150 | 23.45 | 16,655 | 35.06 |
| 1958 | 16,706 | 46.03 | 492 | 1.36 |
| 1954–8 | 70,030 | 34.11 | 25,494 | 12.42 |

*The Registrar's data, subject to the amendments listed in this statistical note, gives the following figures for C.E.G.B. orders (£'000):

| 1954 | £ 4,867 |
|---|---|
| 1955 | 31,354 |
| 1956 | 9,002 |
| 1957 | 11,245 |
| 1958 | 16,758 |
| 1954–8 | 73,226 |

†All these orders in 1957 were placed by the C.E.G.B./S.S.E.B. In other years they were placed by the United Kingdom Atomic Energy Authority, or the Ministry of Supply.

TABLE 1    Generating sets programmed

| Size of set (MW) | No. of sets | | | | | |
|---|---|---|---|---|---|---|
| | 1955 | 1956 | 1957 | 1958 | 1959 | 1960 |
| under 30 | 1 | 2 | 2 | — | 1 | — |
| 30 | 10 | 11 | 10 | 6 | — | — |
| 60 | 19 | 20 | 18 | 12 | 11 | 14 |
| 100, straight | 1 | 3 | 2 | 2 | 2 | — |
| 100, reheat | — | 1 | 1 | — | 2 | 1 |
| 120, reheat | — | — | 2 | 2 | 5 | 7 |
| 200, reheat | — | — | — | — | 1 | 2 |
| | 1961 | 1962 | 1963 | | | |
| 60 | 4 | — | — | | | |
| 100 | 1 | 1 | 2 | | | |
| 120 | 6 | 7 | 3 | | | |
| 200 | 5 | 2 | — | | | |
| 275 | — | 1 | 1 | | | |
| 300 | — | — | 1 | | | |
| 550 | — | — | 1 | | | |

The figures are for 'conventional' plant only, and do not include nuclear plant, or, of course, hydro-electric plant.

*Sources*
1955–60 Report of the (Herbert) Committee of Inquiry into the Electricity Supply Industry (H.M.S.O. Cmd 9672), para. 103.
1961    Central Electricity Authority Annual Report and Accounts 1955–56, para. 107
1962    Central Electricity Authority Annual Report and Accounts 1956–57, para. 104
1963    Central Electricity Authority Annual Report and Accounts 1957–58, para. 103.

*TABLE 2*    Sizes of individual boilers in C.E.A. and C.E.G.B. contracts, 1951—8

| Starting dates of contracts | Average boiler in all contracts | Average boiler in W.T.B.A. contracts | Average boiler in non-W.T.B.A. contracts | Rating of largest boiler in W.T.B.A. contracts | Rating of largest boiler in non-W.T.B.A. contracts |
|---|---|---|---|---|---|
| Year | MW | MW | MW | MW | MW |
| 1951 | 40.5 | 48.4 | 26.3 | 100 | 60 |
| 1952 | 39.4 | 40.2 | 35.4 | 120 | 60 |
| 1953 | 44.9 | 62.5 | 20.2 | 120 | 60 |
| 1954 | 71.4 | 106.6 | 45.0 | 120 | 60 |
| 1955 | 97.1 | 102.3 | 90.0 | 200 | 120 |
| 1956 | 113.3 | 200.0 | 70.0 | 200 | 120 |
| 1957 | 123.1 | 146.7 | 102.9 | 200 | 120 |
| 1958 | 181.8 | 243.3 | 108.0 | 550 | 120 |

*Source:* Statistics agreed between the W.T.B.A. and the Registrar, subject to Appendix 4.1.


*TABLE 3*    The make-up of costs for the four 'manufacturing' members of W.T.B.A.

*Note:* Figures were for the latest accounting year date available for each company, 1957—8. The figures relate only to water-tube boilers coming within the scope of the Association and to ancillary steam-boiler plant or equipment.

| | | %<br>100.00 |
|---|---|---|
| | The contract value of the work done of which | |
| (a) | Total value of materials bought for further processing | 12.36 |
| (b) | Total wages in respect of works labour | 8.84 |
| (c) | Total wages in respect of erection labour | 6.69 |
| (d) | Other wages and salaries excl. design and research staff | 5.66 |
| (e) | Salaries cost of design and research staff | 1.81 |
| (f) | Repairs and maintenance, services and supplies, etc. | 10.88 |
| (g) | Charges allocated to depreciation, obsolescence, replacement | 2.64 |
| (h) | Value of all sub-contracted material bought and supplied | 42.69 |

TABLE 4   Orders placed with W.T.B.A. members

| Year | C.E.G.B. and S.S.E.B. orders, including atomic power stations £'000 | % | Other home orders* £'000 | % | Total overseas orders £'000 | % | Total orders £'000 | % |
|---|---|---|---|---|---|---|---|---|
| 1954 | 5,316 | 19.42 | 10,032 | 36.64 | 12,029 | 43.94 | 27,377 | 100.00 |
| 1955 | 36,393 | 60.98 | 5,128 | 8.59 | 18,156 | 30.42 | 59,677 | 100.00 |
| 1956 | 8,812 | 25.64 | 5,539 | 16.12 | 20,013 | 58.24 | 34,364 | 100.00 |
| 1957 | 27,805 | 58.51 | 1,847 | 3.81 | 17,926 | 37.68 | 47,578 | 100.00 |
| 1958 | 17,198 | 47.39 | 2,856 | 7.87 | 16,236 | 44.74 | 36,290 | 100.00 |
| 1954–8 | 95,524 | 46.53 | 25,402 | 12.38 | 84,360 | 41.09 | 205,286 | 100.00 |

*Includes Northern Ireland Central Station orders (£'000):

| 1954 | 1,255 |
| 1955 | 245 |
| 1956 | 577 |

Source: W.T.B.A. statistics, assembled for this Case. See Appendix 4.1.

TABLE 5  Overseas orders

Overseas orders for Territories within the scope of W.T.B.A.

| Year | Placed with W.T.B.A. members | | Placed with other U.K. boilermakers | | Placed outside U.K.* | | Total of overseas orders within scope | | Orders outside W.T.B.A. scope placed with W.T.B.A. members | Total placed with W.T.B.A. members |
|---|---|---|---|---|---|---|---|---|---|---|
| | £'000 | % | £'000 | % | £'000 | % | £'000 | % | £'000 | £'000 |
| 1954 | 11,807 | 89.40 | 400 | 3.03 | 1,000 | 7.57 | 13,207 | 100.0 | 222 | 12,029 |
| 1955 | 16,904 | 88.02 | 300 | 1.56 | 2,000 | 10.42 | 19,204 | 100.0 | 1,252 | 18,156 |
| 1956 | 18,609 | 74.41 | 2,000 | 8.00 | 4,400 | 17.59 | 25,009 | 100.0 | 1,404 | 20,013 |
| 1957 | 16,590 | 77.41 | 2,940 | 13.72 | 1,900 | 8.87 | 21,430 | 100.0 | 1,336 | 17,926 |
| 1958 | 8,291 | 73.82 | 40 | 0.36 | 2,900 | 25.82 | 11,231 | 100.0 | 7,945 | 16,236 |
| 1954–8 | 72,201 | 80.15 | 5,680 | 6.31 | 12,200 | 13.54 | 90,081 | 100.0 | 12,159 | 84,360 |

*Excl. Russia.

Source: W.T.B.A. statistics, assembled for this Case.

TABLE 6   Nos. of non-C.E.G.B. orders individually worth more than (£'000)

| Year | 150 | 250 | 500 | 750 | 1,000 | 2,000 | 3,000 | 4,000 |
|------|-----|-----|-----|-----|-------|-------|-------|-------|
| 1954* | 29 | 23 | 10 | 7 | 4 | 1 | – | – |
| 1955* | 33 | 20 | 8 | 6 | 3 | 1 | – | – |
| 1956* | 29 | 20 | 12 | 7 | 5 | 2 | 1 | 1 |
| 1957 | 20 | 13 | 7 | 6 | 3 | 2 | 1 | – |
| 1958 | 19 | 11 | 4 | 3 | 2 | – | – | – |

*Incl. the following orders for central power stations in Northern Ireland (£'000):

|  |  |
|------|------|
| 1954 | 1,255 |
| 1955 | 245 |
| 1956 | 577 |

*Source:* W.T.B.A. records.


TABLE 7a   Individual non-C.E.G.B. home orders compared with total value of orders received by individual members, each year 1954–8

| Year | Total non-C.E.G.B. home orders | No. of non-C.E.G.B. home orders | No. of orders in column 3 which were each greater in value than one-fifth of [the total home orders (industrial and central station excl. nuclear stations) plus overseas orders within the scope of the Association, placed with member] | | | | | |
|------|------|------|------|------|------|------|------|------|
|  | £000 |  | No. 1 | No. 2 | No. 3 | No. 4 | No. 5 | No. 6 |
| 1954* | 10,032* | 43* | 0 | 11* | 5* | 10* | 15* | 42* |
| 1955* | 5,128* | 42* | 0 | 26* | 0 | 0 | 42* | 0 |
| 1956* | 5,539* | 35* | 0 | 9* | 1 | 1 | 4* | 16* |
| 1957 | 1,812 | 21 | 0 | 18 | 0 | 1 | 0 | 5 |
| 1958 | 2,856 | 23 | 0 | 16 | 0 | 0 | 10 | 0 |
|  |  | 164 | 0 | 80 | 6 | 12 | 71 | 63 |

*TABLE 7b*    Individual non-C.E.G.B. home and overseas orders compared
with total value of orders received by individual members,
each year 1954—8

| Year | Total non-C.E.G.B. home orders plus total overseas orders within the scope | Total no. of such orders | No. of orders in column 3 which were each greater in value than one-fifth of [the total home orders (industrial and central station excl. nuclear stations) plus overseas orders within the scope of the Association, placed with member] | | | | | |
|------|------|------|------|------|------|------|------|------|
| | £000 | | No. 1 | No. 2 | No. 3 | No. 4 | No. 5 | No. 6 |
| 1954* | 21,839* | 109* | 1 | 17* | 8* | 16* | 27* | 101* |
| 1955* | 22,032* | 135* | — | 65* | — | 3 | 134* | 10 |
| 1956* | 24,148* | 113* | — | 27* | 6 | 8 | 14* | 48* |
| 1957 | 18,402 | 64 | 1 | 55 | 2 | 12 | 10 | 22 |
| 1958 | 11,147 | 70 | 1 | 49 | 1 | 2 | 30 | — |
| | | 491 | 3 | 213 | 17 | 41 | 215 | 181 |

*Incl. the following orders (one each year) for central power stations in Northern
Ireland (£'000)

|      |       |
|------|-------|
| 1954 | 1,255 |
| 1955 | 245   |
| 1956 | 577   |

If these are excluded from the count on the right-hand side of the table, the numbers
marked * should all be reduced by one.

*Source:* W.T.B.A. records

*General Note to Tables 7a and 7b* — Total C.E.G.B. orders in these years were as
follows:

|      | Value (£'000) | Number |
|------|---------------|--------|
| 1954 | 4,867         | 3      |
| 1955 | 31,354        | 21     |
| 1956 | 9,002         | 3      |
| 1957 | 11,245        | 6      |
| 1958 | 16,758        | 4      |

*TABLE 8* W.T.B.A. members annual production of water-tube steam-boiler plant 1952—6

Approximate figures (£'000)

| Year | Home business Value of material (incl. bought-out material delivered during year) | Value of erection work carried out during year | Total value of home work | Overseas Business Value of material (incl. bought-out material delivered during the year to the point of f.o.b.) | Total of previous columns |
|---|---|---|---|---|---|
| 1952 | 26,147 | 4,252 | 30,399 | 15,272 | 45,671 |
| 1953 | 27,883 | 4,090 | 31,973 | 15,910 | 47,883 |
| 1954 | 30,748 | 4,385 | 35,138 | 15,129 | 50,262 |
| 1955 | 36,982 | 5,345 | 42,327 | 17,260 | 59,587 |
| 1956 | 39,430 | 5,775 | 45,205 | 12,606 | 57,811 |
| 1952—6 | 161,190 | 23,847 | 185,037 | 76,177 | 261,214 |

*Note:* Without special work on overseas accounts it was not possible to compile figures for the value of erection and other work carried out in the overseas countries where boilers were supplied.
*Source:* W.T.B.A. Statistics assembled for this Case.

*TABLE 9*  Distribution of C.E.G.B./C.E.A./B.E.A. contracts 1951–8

| | 1 | 2 | 3 | 4 | 5 | 6 | 7 | 8 | 9 |
|---|---|---|---|---|---|---|---|---|---|
| Year | Total allocated contracts MW | Col. 1 as % of all contracts (col. 5) % | Total competitive contracts MW | Col. 3 as % of all contracts (col. 5) % | Total all contracts MW | Total contracts placed with W.T.B.A. members MW | Col. 6 as % of all contracts (col. 5) % | Total contracts placed with non-W.T.B.A. members MW | Col. 8 as % of all contracts (col. 5) % |
| 1951 | 2024 | 100.0 | — | — | 2024 | 1550 | 76.6 | 474 | 23.4 |
| 1952 | 1658 | 95.6 | 76 | 4.4 | 1734 | 1486 | 85.7 | 248 | 14.3 |
| 1953 | 797 | 74.0 | 280 | 26.0 | 1077 | 875 | 81.2 | 202 | 18.8 |
| 1954 | 500 | 100.0 | — | — | 500 | 320 | 64.0 | 180 | 36.0 |
| 1955 | 1050 | 28.5 | 2640 | 71.5 | 3690 | 2250 | 61.0 | 1440 | 39.0 |
| 1956 | 560 | 41.2 | 800 | 58.8 | 1360 | 800 | 58.8 | 560 | 41.2 |
| 1957 | 960 | 60.0 | 640 | 40.0 | 1600 | 880 | 55.0 | 720 | 45.0 |
| 1958 | 660 | 33.0 | 1340 | 67.0 | 2000 | 1460 | 73.0 | 540 | 27.0 |

| | 10 | 11<br>Contracts Placed with W.T.B.A. Members | 12 | 13 | 14 | 15<br>Contracts Placed with non-W.T.B.A. Firms | 16 | 17 |
|---|---|---|---|---|---|---|---|---|
| Year | Allocated contracts MW | Col. 10 as % of total W.T.B.A. contracts (col. 6) % | Competitive contracts MW | Col. 12 as % of total W.T.B.A. contracts (col. 6) % | Allocated contracts MW | Col. 14 as % of total non-W.T.B.A. contracts (col. 8) % | Competitive contracts MW | Col. 16 as % of total non-W.T.B.A. contracts (col. 8) % |
| 1951 | 1550 | 100.0 | – | – | 474 | 100.0 | – | – |
| 1952 | 1410 | 94.9 | 76 | 5.1 | 248 | 100.0 | – | – |
| 1953 | 695 | 79.4 | 180 | 20.6 | 102 | 50.5 | 100 | 49.5 |
| 1954 | 320 | 100.0 | – | – | 180 | 100.0 | – | – |
| 1955 | 990 | 44.0 | 1260 | 56.0 | 60 | 4.2 | 1380 | 95.8 |
| 1956 | – | – | 800 | 100.0 | 560 | 100.0 | – | – |
| 1957 | 240 | 27.3 | 640 | 72.7 | 720 | 100.0 | – | – |
| 1958 | 120 | 8.2 | 1340 | 91.8 | 540 | 100.0 | – | – |

*Note:* W.T.B.A. contracts are dated by the year in which the member received instructions to proceed in the view of the Association. The few cases where the Registrar would choose another date are referred to in Appendix 4.1. There is also one case where I follow the Registrar in treating a contract as an allocated contract although the industry puts forward grounds for regarding it as having been awarded under competitive price conditions. See Appendix 4.1.

*Source:* Statistics agreed with the Registrar by the W.T.B.A. with the exceptions of items covered by Appendix 4.1.

*TABLE 10*     C.E.G.B. commissioning programmes

| Programme year | Total new capacity (MW) | Conventional capacity (MW) | Nuclear capacity (MW) |
|---|---|---|---|
| 1961 | 2445 | 1870 | 575 |
| 1962 | 2350 | 1850 | 500 |
| 1963 | 1820 | 1570 | 250 |
| 1964 | 1730 | 1230 | 500 |
| 1965 | 2120 | 970 | 1150 |
| 1966 | 2150 | 650 | 1500 |
| 1967 | 2300 | 1100 | 1200 |

APPENDIX 4.2

**Note on proof of evidence of Professor Pool**

Professor Pool contrasts the effects of the tendering arrangements of the W.T.B.A. with what would happen in 'unrestricted competition'. (I note that the phrase several times used to denote those arrangements — 'collusive tendering' — seems inappropriate as tending to imply that there is collusion as to the prices of all W.T.B.A. tenders in contracts affected by those arrangements.) His conclusions are vitiated by his not taking adequate account of some important facts about the industry and circumstances in which it is operating.

The facts about the industry and the circumstances to which I refer are as follows:

(i)   The structure of the market on the demand side.

(ii)  The effect of the ways in which the C.E.G.B. has chosen to exercise its market power on the commercial position of members of the W.T.B.A.

(iii) The probable shortage of demand in relation to the industry's productive capacity for several years ahead.

(iv)  The economic characteristics of the product.

(v)   The relative importance of overhead costs, and particularly of cash overhead costs.

(vi)  The relative fewness of the suppliers with the resulting condition of oligopoly.

(vii) The characteristics of the contracts by which the products are ordered.

Nos. (i), (iv), (vi) and (vii) make it inappropriate, in my view, for the working of the industry and the effects of the Agreement to be analysed in terms of theoretical perfect competition (which is the analysis underlying Professor Pool's tendency to refer competitive prices to costs) and the imposition of simple monopolistic collusion on this condition; if he chose to analyse these in terms of 'imperfect' or 'monopolistic' competition analysis then he could not derive his conclusions about the efficiencies of individual businesses under unrestricted competition.

Nos. (i), (iv), (v), (vi) and (vii) similarly, make it incorrect to refer prices on particular tenders to the normal levels of costs and efficiencies of individual businesses (as Professor Pool does in his discussion of the dispersion of the prices in individual contracts).

It is, I think, a major defect in Professor Pool's approach to the industry that his analysis is completely long-run in character, especially in view of the fact of excess capacity which is likely to persist for some years (if not for so long as the 'coming decades' to which Professor Pool looks in his forecasts of demand).

Professor Pool ignores some important aspects of (i) (the sizes of individual orders and their fewness at any one time, with the resulting market power of customers generally, quite apart from that of the C.E.G.B.), and he takes no account of (ii), (iii), (iv), (v), (vi) and (vii): this seems to me sufficient to explain the fact that he sees 'no reason why the lower competitive prices that would follow the removal of the restrictions should be unprofitably low'.

# 5 Some Economic Aspects of the Building Industry

## INTRODUCTION

### MEMBERSHIP OF THE SEMINAR

An industry research seminar was specially set up by the Building Research Station 1963–5. The members were variously academic economists, staff of the Research Station, and members of the then Building Research Board, twelve in all. Their names and affiliations at the time were: Mr P. W. S. Andrews, Chairman, Nuffield College; Professor G. A. Barnard, Imperial College; Mr D. Bishop, Building Research Station; Mr J. R. Britten, Secretary, Building Research Station; Miss E. Brunner, Nuffield College; Mr T. A. B. Corley, University of Reading; Mr B. Cullen, Building Research Station: Mr J. B. Dick, Building Research Station; Mr M. S. Feldstein, Nuffield College; Mr J. S. Flemming, Oriel College; Mr J. Musgrove, Bartlett School of Architecture; Dr J. C. Weston, Building Research Station. Lord Llewellyn Davies was a member of the original group but other commitments prevented his attendance at later meetings. Professor Bela Gold of the University of Pittsburgh, on leave at Oxford, attended five meetings and Sir Frederick Lea, then Director of Building Research, B.R.S., was present at one meeting.

### SCOPE AND METHOD OF THE RESEARCH

The seminar's research into economic aspects of the building and construction industry was based upon interviews with selected businessmen and used methods developed, in particular, in the Oxford University graduate seminar in economics of industries, of which six of the members had had experience and of which P. W. S. Andrews was for many years chairman. This was in no sense a 'survey' type of investigation. Attention was concentrated on individual businesses. The seminar had moreover a limited programme because it had an exploratory function so far as the Building Research Station was concerned, to show how far this kind of research group could get insight into the role of the building firm (as an extension of the existing B.R.S. work in the economic field, which concentrates, for example, on the efficiency of particular building operations). The aim here was to seek guidelines which would provide additional background for B.R.S.'s existing research programme, and indicate projects for future research, and which themselves would spring from economic analysis of the building industry at the level of the individual firm. In the interest of useful theoretical generalisation, the general area of study was limited to decision-making with regard to costing and pricing, and, within this area, the seminar came to concentrate on the pricing of (selective) tenders.[1]

In a year's programme of meetings, the seminar met on sixteen occasions and studied seven businesses. Meetings at which individual businessmen were interviewed alternated with those attended only by members of the seminar, at which the meetings with businessmen were discussed. Each businessman-meeting lasted approximately two hours and was followed by a dinner at which discussion continued less formally. Individual note-taking was the rule and helped to sharpen personal assessments of the business evidence; at the same time, our private discussions and the preparation of this report were alike considerably helped by the minutes kept by Mr Britten as secretary and by the general report which he prepared.

Appendix 5.1 gives the 'agenda headings' used at each meeting with businessmen. At such a meeting discussion ranged freely under the guidance of the businessman concerned, who had been told of these headings in advance. He discussed any questions in the detail which he thought relevant, and raised any matters which interested him under any heading without necessarily discussing every item on the agenda. Each therefore had the opportunity to develop those features which he thought to be important. (In due course, each was also sent an earlier draft of this report and provided helpful comments in the light of our work as a whole.)

BUSINESSES STUDIED[2]

The seven businesses were chosen on the basis of a diversity of characteristics which were thought relevant to the purposes of the inquiry, but the sample was not intended to be a representative cross-section of the industry. Before saying more about them, it may be useful to comment on their 'representativeness' from the point of view of theoretical work. The businesses were *selected* to represent in diverse ways such elements as size, variety of financial and managerial control, and variety of work and diversity of location. In the selection of these as well as in the interpretation of evidence and other matters affecting the balance of our discussions, and therefore of this report, the seminar was helped, of course, by the considerable acquaintance with the building industry which some members had. Not less were we helped by the individual business-man's view of what might be peculiar to his business and what would be common points for other businesses which he knew as competitors or otherwise. In theoretical analysis, we set factors which are special to, and important for, building into the usual setting based on assumptions that businesses will seek to be profitable and try to avoid losses. We may hope to have gained insight into these special building factors from the research of the seminar but the analysis, being theoretical, has independent validity; the factors clearly have importance in themselves and the 'representa-tiveness' of the analysis is to be judged in terms of the cogency of the argument with regard to their effects.[3] Given the basic assumptions, the argument should be valid whenever policy, business or public, is considering the factors to which the analysis gives prominence.

Both small family businesses and large public companies were included, as was civil engineering and specialist services, in addition to general building. The smallest firm we interviewed concentrates on repairs and conversions, and such activities are also carried out by some of the larger businesses. At the same time, our businessmen included those who came from large concerns in which civil engineering construction of the largest scale was as important as building narrowly defined. The businessmen interviewed were all at the policy-making level in their companies; the degree to which they were still involved in the day to day running of their organisations depended on the size of their business, but those not now so engaged had had such experience at some time.

Taking up briefly matters which are dealt with later, it may be said that the diverse histories of these businesses are themselves illustrations of how organically linked the whole building—construction complex is in terms of the supply of enterprise, e.g. one company which had started in speculative housing is now a major business in civil engineering. Our witnesses varied greatly in the amount of sub-contracting given out or taken on. Whilst there was no apparent tendency for the size of business or the nature of the work to inhibit the giving of sub-contracts, at both extremes of the size range there were restrictions on taking them. The smallest firm put out work on sub-contract but did not itself do such work for others; a medium-sized concern was organised in separate departments which were free to find their own balance of work in or outside the business by sub-contracts both ways; the largest firms might put a lot of work out on sub-contract or have a policy of doing everything themselves, but apparently undertook sub-contracting only in a specialist field. A different but related matter arises with the plant departments, where availability to others on a hire basis was seen by medium-sized businesses as being important for economic working.

MATTERS DISCUSSED

The focus of interest led to a great deal being learnt about the business environment in which commercial policies are decided and tenders are made. Because the businessmen were not normally involved in subordinate procedures, and because the seminar was concerned with general principles, the mechanism of preparing estimates was seldom discussed in detail. We found a variety of practice in the allocation of establishment and overhead charges and in the way provisions for these were included in estimates. The procedures involved in adjusting such estimates, on the other hand, to allow for the updating of basic quotations, special contingencies, etc., seemed to be broadly similar. The question of the final 'adjudication' of estimates, involving the top-level decisions which convert them into quoted prices, was discussed in detail.

When attitudes to growth were dicussed, economic factors common to the industry were mixed with others which were more idiosyncratic. The ways in which builders obtained work were of particular interest because of the relevance both to the possibility of growth and to the market position of the individual business; we discussed speculative construction, and package-deal contracts, as well as contracts obtained by competitive tender. Six out of the seven businesses had 'small works' departments; although these might be mentioned because of difficulties in their organisation, stress was placed on the value of their continuous connexions with customers out of which the occasional, substantial contract might come. When discussing growth and the obtaining and organisation of work, there was frequent reference to the importance of supervisory staff around whom practical planning was organised. We mention this the more especially because practically every businessman came back to this under the last heading of the agenda as a 'major problem' or the major problem facing him in the development of his business — a significant pointer for the Construction Industry Training Board.

Turning to the content of this report, undertakings as to confidentiality prevent us from discussing individual businesses in continuous detail. The flexibility of approach by businessmen and ourselves to our discussions via the agenda, and the diversity of emphasis from one business to another, also prevent any neat tabular summary of the evidence which we have taken. All members of the seminar, however, are very conscious of the benefit from the frank discussions which we have been able to have under the umbrella of confidentiality, and especially in keeping generalisations under check from the details of particular cases. The general conclusions drawn in the seminar from discussions of the matters mentioned, and other factors then brought up, have been used in the second and third sections of this report, which discuss economic aspects of the building and construction industries, with special reference to the activity of individual businesses. As already indicated, however, within this broader discussion there was a sharper focus on the contract tender system, and the fourth section of this report is concerned with this. Although only a proporton of the output of the construction industry is sold by competitive tender, it is an important proportion and there seem likely to be significant general effects on the whole economy of the industry. Some speculations about this are offered in the fifth and final section.

## ECONOMIC ANALYSIS OF THE BUILDING INDUSTRY
### 'BUILDING' AS AN ECONOMIC ACTIVITY

So far we have followed popular language in referring to 'building' or 'construction', knowing that anyone would recognise the kind of businesses to which we are referring and the kind of work which they are to be thought of as doing. In practice, any particular business may well be doing other things as well. For the economic analysis of building as such it is necessary to be more precise about the activities which are to be given special consideration. As it happens, the Standard Industrial Classification which is used for official statistics draws the distinctions which we would follow: under 'Building and construction', it *includes* building, civil engineering and open-cast mining work, and the work of sub-contractors in these fields; but it *excludes* the supply and distribution of building materials. Within this general boundary, the kind of work which businesses are doing will be much the same from a management point of view — excavating and other work on site and the preparation for construction, and the assembly of materials and components into a structure.

What a building firm is doing at any one time may be narrower in scope because of its size, its organisation or the geographical area where it works, or by deliberate choice; as a long-term matter, however, there will be no fundamental technical or managerial limitation within the boundaries of the definition, where, accordingly, organisation and enterprise may be thought to have a plastic freedom to move in response to commercial incentives. This plasticity of constructional business is enhanced by the freedom to use sub-contractors and to act as sub-contractors to others. No matter how narrow its present scope, or how humble its stature, a sub-contracting firm coming within the definition is in the building industry from an economic point of view and has the basis to develop independent building work and so is technically as free to move within the industry as are other builders.

Taking building as defined, there is a clear difference from the ordinary run of manufacturing in which goods are made in quantities of standard specifications in given factories, typically in advance of actual demand, and offered at makers' prices, some stages away from the consumers to whom they will be distributed; that kind of manufacturing industry has provided the pattern for the usual analysis of business in economic theory. By contrast, building is rather a 'bespoke' industry; jobs are typically 'one-off' and non-routinised. Even in the case of speculative building where a builder offers 'his' houses for sale, a large part of the work will be affected by peculiarities of sites, operations are discontinuous and have to move from site to site, and what is offered at any one site may be affected by the changing cost of land, etc.; moreover, the final product may even be finished according to customers' specifications.

To come back to the question of the analysis of manufacturing industry, it is true that a few industries (such as that supplying heavy electrical generating equipment) have much in common with building as we see it; but this simply means that such an industry will be better analysed on the basis of a 'building-type' model than with a 'manufacturing' model, and there has been little analytical discussion of such a type. The exclusion of the industries making building supplies from the economic analysis of building as such is directly justifiable because their economics are typical of manufacturing; there is also the organisational, empirical reason that they are characteristically run as separate industries.[4]

In general, an activity is to be thought of as part of building only if it is typically too intimately involved with building operations to be separated. The details of any such interrelationship must be expected to change over time, but the principle of analytical separation must be kept. Thus, at one time, even bricks might be best made on site for the job in hand, but the development of a separate industry offering standard products to a general market has removed them to outside manufacture from the analytical point of view as well. Standard joinery, such as mass-produced doors and window frames, has gone the same way; a large builder who in fact does such work for himself is to be seen as choosing to invest in an activity which will have to meet the external test of prices and services from regular manufacturers. When it comes to 'custom-built' elements, such as some joinery or special pre-cast concrete work, however, the specifications are so affected by the individual job that arranging for them is part of normal building activity.

Contemporary developments in connexion with 'system' building may seem to be an in-between case, but it will be useful to draw the same basic distinctions between building and the supply of standardised components available on a general market. Where, as may be at present, a builder is developing a system in his contracts, his whole activity on the component side will be closely related to his contracts, and the 'pricing' of these components, as any other element in his operations, will be discretionary; he will get or lose a contract on his price for the job as a whole. Particularly in view of the present apparent diversity of systems, one may foresee, however, a great reduction in the number of competing, genuinely different, systems; so that there should develop a general market for the component elements of systems whose manufacturers will specialise on them, individual builders in general buying what they need.

In summary, to return to the main point of this sub-section, building as such – which will in practice be the distinctive activity of building firms – may be claimed to be economically distinctive, not because different *kinds* of factors influence any given class of business decisions, but because the circumstances which especially characterise building may well lead to *a different degree*, or quality, of response to those factors from that to be expected in ordinary manufacturing. Thus, to take the example of the degree of mechanisation, a subject often discussed with reference to building, the major factors which a business will look at when deciding how far to go will be costs, taking into account wages and the prices of pieces of equipment; but, if one had a situation where such cost factors were equally favourable to further mechanisation in building and in some ordinary kind of manufacturing, special features of the building industry might well lead to a lower level of actual mechanisation so far as building operations were concerned. To explain this example further would take one too far into later discussion at this point, though to mention it gives a preliminary glimpse of the kind of reasons why this paper has been written. Before coming to such matters in relation to the individual building firm, we have to consider in more detail the general characteristics of the building industry, and particularly how they bear on its competitiveness, which has indeed itself been foreshadowed in the definition expounded in this sub-section.

## THE COMPETITIVENESS OF BUILDING

We list features of the building industry, some of which are specially noticeable in it, and even though others may be found in a number of industries, they give a distinctive character to the general economics of building, and notably to the competition which the individual business both generates and experiences:

(i) The variety of specifications of work which will be required in a changing mixture by the jobs which come in course of trade to any business, and which it must be prepared to undertake as a regular matter.

(ii) (Consequentially) the differing organisation and facilities which may be required on different jobs, and for which the set-up of the business must provide.

(iii) The wide range of sizes of jobs carried out by practically any business (even if the replacement of tap washers by a small works department be set only against the other jobs which that department does).

(iv) The large size which some individual jobs will have in relation to the total turnover of a business.

(v) The considerable time which building works may take to complete – and the further substantial time lag which may elapse between completion and payment (of which the withholding of 'retention money' is only one aspect).

(vi) The serial nature of building activity – jobs characteristically have to be completed in successive stages with different, and different proportions of, 'inputs' of material and human resources at each stage.

(vii) The employment of men in relatively small groups, with discontinuous work on individual jobs.

(viii) The large part of the work force which necessarily, or at least characteristically, shifts between firms and some of which is 'nomadic' in experience and temperament.

(ix) The continual shift of production to new sites.

(x) The diversity and bulk of materials and components which must be on hand and on site at the right time, and which must be organised not only with regard to operations but also to security, materials costs forming a large proportion of total costs.

(xi) (Partly consequential on other factors) the importance of circulating capital needed to finance current operations, wages, materials and salaries, etc., and the relatively low level of fixed-capital investment in relation to turnover, even when account is taken of the scope for large differences between businesses with regard to fixed capitalisation and the increased importance of fixed capital in the larger businesses and in some sectors of the industry.

(xii) The special reasons for uncertainty of operations, including cost estimating, due to variations in site and weather conditions.

(xiii) The role of the architect and other professional specialists, *vis-à-vis* both builder and client.[5]

The first three factors are a special cause of building being characteristically so multi-product an industry. It is generally true that it is difficult to fit multi-product businesses neatly into ordinary theoretical frameworks, but a building firm is a special sort of multi-product firm. As Mr Flemming put it, in a memorandum to the seminar:

> a building firm is very peculiar in that it sells unique bundles of its different products. (This is also the case with grocers but they do not do as much processing as do builders; food products firms sell their products independently, the elements of any particular order are not as closely tied together both on production and sale, as are those of the builder.) We do not call a one-model washing machine company multi-product on account of the numerous components that go into a single washing machine because in any one model the balance of the different components is fixed.

We shall consider the economics of the individual firm more especially in the next section of this report, but one quality which it must have is obvious from many of the factors we have listed and is important for the competitiveness of the whole building industry: this is a flexibility of organisation to cope with the operations which different jobs will combine in different proportions and require to different extents. A builder, working with his given capital and management set-up, and his nucleus of labour and equipment, etc. (a concept which is further examined in the next section), can readily take on a relatively wide range of jobs within whatever area is convenient to him. At the same time the relative importance of current finance in total capital, and other features of the industry (such as the availability of trade credit for the short-term finance of materials and supplies), make it easier to provide for growth than in industries where fixed capital is more important, and material costs less (and output is not generally sold in advance of production).

The other side of these aspects is that the individual can readily compete for work over the whole range of his possible activity, and the time lag of building arrangements in particular makes it possible to grow at the larger-project end of the range, if that is attractive. Given time to change, and to add to the scale of his organisation, the individual builder can of course enlarge his business as a whole, and, with increased scale, will come changes in the kind of work which he can take on, which will further broaden the scope for his competition. In general, there will be a more or less continuous overlap of competitive interest from individual businesses over successive ranges of size, and for any one job this competition will arise from businesses which may differ considerably in the precise kinds of work which they are currently doing.

The point of these organisational matters, looking at the industry as a whole, is that it is relatively easy for businesses to penetrate one another's markets. To use a concept of one of the present authors, this is to say that 'cross-entry' is easy in this industry;[6] and the time lags involved are probably a good deal less for substantial movement in building than in a good many other industries, where it will tend to be a longer-run affair. If some parts of the building market are somewhat protected by the goodwill of clients towards previous contractors, and of architects towards those whose reputation they 'know', development and growth in some suitable (economically speaking, adjacent) work area may well give an apparent newcomer the status to compete for a 'try', and this kind of extension of business will be helped by the widespread tendency of clients to seek alternative estimates, together with the general use of competitive tenders by important clients in major sections of the market, both practices being encouraged by the uneven occurrence and individuality of building works.

This concept of cross-entry extends the normal theoretical idea of new 'entry' in the sense of the entry of businesses which are new to the general industry, which has always been seen to have important implications for the competitiveness of an industry; but to restrict new competition in a particular market to such entry has often led to an undervaluation of the force of competition itself. In the case of building, however, even in such a restricted sense, 'new entry' is itself 'easy' in the technical economic sense. The general talent which is required for responsible management seems widely available from people with subordinate experience, and the industry offers a good deal of scope for any who wish to chance their arm in independent business. Because of the very diversity of jobs, and the range of their size and type, such people may see useful prospects for relatively small capital, and a successful start anywhere is a bridgehead for further growth.[7]

The fundamental idea in the usual economic analysis of a competitive industry, producing given commodities, is that prices will be determined in the counterbalancing of the pressures of demand and the responses of supply. Short period, prices will move with the flux of competition as businesses experience varying utilisation of existing plant capacities. Longer term, customers will have to pay prices which will cover all costs of whatever quantities they demand at those prices, or capacities will fall off until a more durable equilibrium is reached. Equally, if prices rise above this level, the extension of capacity will bring them back to it. This is how 'entry' comes into the picture as the fundamental regulator of the longer-run supply situation.[8]

The notion of given commodities sold at market prices is, however, difficult to apply directly to building work, in view of the diversity of individual building projects. For abstract analysis, this difficulty may be bypassed by thinking in terms of the basic kinds of operation (excavating, walling, etc.) which go into a building as though these themselves were standardisable marketable commodities. Building consisting of the combination of such operations, we may think of market forces as directly affecting the prices obtainable per measured unit of them, and so as indirectly determining the price for a completed structure. A builder when deciding what he will quote for a particular job may be thought of as trying to use his various skills and resources to best advantage, and settling the price at which he will compete in terms of a (weighted) sum of market opportunities. Matters may be left here for present broad theoretical purposes; but if we were thinking more narrowly of particular sectors of the building market, or of particular types of building within a sector, we should have to allow for some combinations of operations being in readier supply than others. At any one time, businesses which have facilities for some combinations of operations may offer a larger capacity in relation to demand than businesses with facilities for others; in the longer run increased supplies of some combinations may be less readily available than those of others. (This has application to some contemporary discussion of the economics of labour-only sub-contracting.) However, abstract though it is, this idea of the markets for basic building operations also appears to have some real significance.

Our witnesses stressed not only their 'feel' for the movement of the market for the complete building projects for which they were quoting, but also an awareness — and the importance of being aware — of the movement of prices for constituent elements of the kind we have been discussing. More, they explained regular procedures for 'costing' such items in tenders on the basis of a sensitivity to the changes in the corresponding detailed market positions. In short, as an economist may see it, to use this 'feel' for the building market is to cut beneath, and to believe that some real regularity underlies, the considerable variety and flux of actual building prices, as settled from day to day for the various individual building jobs in which the actual market is organised. Our very practical witnesses certainly took some such position as an element in the formation of business policy. (For example: the witness who had 'gone out for' buildings with concrete work because their prices seemed to offer particular opportunity for his special skills and their further development — 'going out' for such work necessarily involved deliberately quoting on the keen side in relation to jobs on offer.)

The economist's interest of course goes into deeper abstraction than the businessman's. The businessman, having to operate successfully in the changes of the actual world, is especially sensitive to the movements in day to day possibilities resulting from temporary changes in conditions. An economist can handle such conditions only in the most general fashion and will get more help from the businessman in seeing what has happened than he can offer in explaining what is happening. He will, however, hope to be more helpful in the analysis of the longer-term trends of prices which result from less temporary changes in fundamental conditions, in technology and market organisation, and so on. And, as already suggested, the economist will be in companionship with the businessman who is looking ahead as a 'policy' matter, thinking about, say, his management training problems and programmes, the capital equipment he wants, or the sectors of the market which he will cultivate.

Businessmen develop such general ideas because they find them a useful guide through the flux of everyday life. In practice, any such ideal tendencies have to be discerned through the scatter of actual prices. In this scatter, we may distinguish two elements, which may be seen as divergences from underlying trends. First, there are mere chance divergencies, one way or the other; second there will be more systematic, though none the less temporary, movements away from longer-term trends. Builders competing for work are not simply guessing at the movement of abstract values; they are putting in prices with a view to getting as much work as they need at the best returns they think they can achieve, where generally it will be the lowest quotation which will get the individual job.

In so far as all competitors are in much the same position and interpret the market the same way, they will tend to hit prices at about the same level with only random discrepancies, and prices will reflect shorter-term trends up or down. But individual builders will differ greatly in current circumstances and given jobs will have diverse attractions. The bid a builder makes will therefore be higher when he does not want a particular job so much as his competitors, or would find it more costly to carry out; and it will be lower when he has special reasons for wanting the job at the time when it comes on offer. In competitive bids, therefore, the low bids may decide contracts, but the range of quotations, in which builders act on their knowledge of current prices generally, will give more information about the general market. In deciding his bid, as just implied, the individual builder in his assessment of the trends of prices must allow for the range of price quotations which will emerge from the market process.

For practical purposes as well as abstract analysis, therefore, one must allow for this fuzziness of application of theoretical ideas. The basic idea of equilibrium *price* has to be translated into ideas of normal *averages and ranges of prices*. We return to this matter when we discuss contract tendering in particular, and we shall see there how the competitive procedures of building will control the movement of quoted prices through feedback from actual prices in estimates — and thus be reflected back into the ideas of the current ranges of price with which builder and client alike will approach the quoting for fresh work. An assessment of the tendering system in general will then bring us to questions of its repercussions for the organisation of the industry as a whole and for prices in other sectors of the market. But the general conclusion of competitive theory as outlined at the beginning of this sub-section will still be valid: the prices set by the building market taken as a whole will still reflect the shorter-term variance of basic economic factors and in the long run they will be determined by the costs at which adequate capacity can be maintained. In a competitive industry, there is no magic by which lower price trends may be conjured up — though there is room for questions about the possibility of changes of market procedures having beneficial effects on price trends through making it possible for necessary resources to be economised or organised more cheaply. Such questions are given the greater practical scope by reason of a feature of the industry which was not mentioned in the earlier list — the large part of its output which is sold to public authorities of one sort or another, and of which a substantial part is amenable to central control.

Of course, such matters of public policy do not lessen the importance of questions of individual business efficiency, the importance of adoption of new methods, etc., but in a competitive industry one can assume that pressures within the industry will favour their adoption, subject to the overall constraints of the market and administrative background which the analysis of the individual business must take for granted. With this proviso, we turn now to a discussion of the internal economy of the building firm.

## THE INTERNAL ECONOMY OF THE BUILDING FIRM
### THE NUCLEUS ORGANISATION
The range of opportunity on the demand side of building, and the intrinsic flexibility required of the firm on the supply side, have been stressed as the setting for the competition which characterises the industry. Turning, however, to the individual firm, some settledness of character is a fundamental fact to be recognised in the economic analysis. Our witnesses saw their own businesses, and discussed competitors, in terms of characteristics (location, market connexions and organisational set-up) which were stable enough at any given time to be important factors in the impact and operation of the business in the market. Watching a management as it takes current decisions and frames future policy, an economist can see the 'character' of a business as being essentially a matter

of where its activity is aimed within the choices that are open to it and of it having the organisation to further those aims, whilst at the same time it is aware of the influence which its own history and past policies may have had in determining the constraints within which choice is exercised. The seminar came to see 'character' as being embodied in the nucleus-organisation of a business.[9]

The nucleus organisation of a business is the whole cadre of human resources, labour as well as management, of capital equipment and of working capital, which management will keep available despite fluctuations in activity in order to preserve the business's character. Given the size of a business, the precise content of its nucleus will be determined by what it generally builds and how it generally carries out such building. Decisions 'how' are choices between available techniques and equipment and will generally change with growth (or decline) of firm as well as with changes in the kind of building done; but such changes will generally take time to affect the situation greatly, and at any one time the business's nucleus organisation may be taken as given.

We comment further on the human resources in the nucleus in order to stress some special features of the building industry. It is a familiar idea in economics that a business will have a given, overhead, management and capitalisation; what is unusual is to see *labour* as an overhead when one is constructing general models, and it is normally treated as entirely variable costs.[10] It could be said that one need not be distracted in general-purpose models by the fact that much labour in industries such as chemicals is overhead not variable cost, because their situation is dominated by the fixed capital to which overhead labour could be regarded as a secondary concomitant. A building firm, however, if it is to continue as the kind of business which it is, will have to provide for a nucleus of labour which is much larger than that which is unavoidable overhead on strict accounting; in the same way it will have to keep its management nucleus together in the face of temporary fluctuations, and that nucleus itself will have to consist of more people than those who would be needed if the business went on doing the same jobs all the time.

Looked at this way, even though building is not an industry where fixed capital overheads are especially heavy, the economics of the firm will be dominated by its overhead costs, and that the more because a large part of the overheads will be 'paying-out cost',[11] since the human part of the nucleus has to be paid continually; these paying-out, in contrast to capital, overheads, must no less than current variable costs proper be covered by current cash receipts, even in short-run operation, or cash reserves will be correspondingly depleted.

To come from abstract analysis back to reality, if turnover drops badly the drain on cash may force a cut in the organisation, but there will be reluctance to make such a cut because reinvestment will be needed to build the organisation up again. It takes time to get together the groups of people, used to working together in and with various levels of management and carrying out work the 'right' way. In day to day operations the need to spread the burden of overheads adds force to the drive to keep the nucleus organisation continuously employed.

We have said that management is ordinarily thought of as overhead; one thing which makes it a relatively heavy cost in building is the necessity for management to be so continuously involved in the detail of operation – in the operational control and supervision which is required by the features already mentioned as notable in this industry, such as the uniqueness of the individual products, and the lumpiness, serial organisation, and transitory location of building works. Even at site level, and certainly on larger jobs, local management is more closely related to higher decision levels than is foremanship in ordinary industry. There is also far less routine pricing than in industries producing runs of standard products. Estimating and pricing usually involve directors closely or, in the very big firm, come up at least to the level of the regional manager, who may or may not be a director. The importance of current control of costs, and the need to get the maximum help from present experience in assessing future costs, themselves involve management in much post-accounting detail. Further, it must be remembered that the way the building market works requires the individual business to estimate for much more work than it will actually get, so that the organisation here will be related to quotations and tenders rather than contracts.

BUILDING COSTS

The questions discussed here are the effects on the costs of a building firm of (i) changes in output activity, (ii) the size of the individual building project, (iii) change in the size scale of operations for which the firm is organised. The discussion is concerned only with broad tendencies – not less when we turn around and ask about (iv) the implications for market analysis of relevant aspects of the idiosyncratic character of the individual business and of the accidents of its situation, both of which will affect actual costs and may be important in its development. We do not even go into detail as to what is meant by 'costs'; very much of what is needed for discussion of the general economics of building may be taken without worrying about the precise definition, and all that need be stipulated for the use of cost generalisations in later market analysis is that 'costs' should be taken at current values, rather than historical values, should these differ.[12]

## Effects of changing activity

The use of the term 'activity' rather than the usual 'output' hints at the complication for measurement which results from the non-homogeneity of building output and the varying time scales of business works. Basically, one avoids this by thinking in terms of a business all of whose activities are kept in balance to minimise its costs and which always works only within the same range of jobs. In this way the size of output may be kept separate from other matters affecting costs. Such completely standard production is so untypical of building that one may boggle at it. To take account of changes in the 'mix' and yet discuss changing activity in a single dimension, one could instead think in terms of overall output being measured, in index-number fashion, by some kind of weighted sum of the operational units which go into actual jobs, as explained on page 130. This is how the problem would have to be faced in statistical work, and is no more than ought to be done for a multi-product firm anyway. For the kind of general view of costs taken here, the realistic reader must imagine some such standardisation of measurement of output; he will still, however, have to accept the idea of a business which does not change its capital equipment or its managerial organisation as its output activity goes up or down — a necessary abstraction if one is to consider the effects of changes in output separately from the effects of growth of the business.

Taking the managerial set-up as given, it would be perverse unreality not to presume that at any one time a business will be organised, not for some particular output, but for the range of outputs which its management would expect as normal. It would be especially perverse to do so for building which is so subject to short-term changes in activity. The general assumption that a business is organised to cope with some particular range of output, may be taken to entail that, *per unit of output*, average direct costs (the costs of materials and labour actually going into individual jobs) will be more or less constant, the *total* of such direct costs varying directly with output over the planned range of the latter, provided that the variety of jobs in itself does not differ seriously from that for which the business is organised.[13]

It also follows that, over the 'planned' range of output, overhead costs (the costs of capital equipment and management, etc.) will be more or less fixed *in total*, and therefore average overhead costs per unit will fall asymptotically with output. Supposing a business to be somewhere in its planning range, falls of output will, therefore, cause average total costs per unit (the sum of average direct costs and average overhead costs) to rise with increasing steepness as output falls: equally, as output rises, average total costs will fall, though with decreasing steepness.

So far, the picture is one fairly typical for manufacturing in general, apart from the special incidence of fluctuations. But building, as already remarked on pages 133–4, although not a low-overheads industry on balance, has relatively low fixed-capital costs but relatively high management overheads. The incidence of these latter 'paying-out' overheads is, moreover, magnified by another factor affecting direct costs which our simple picture has not allowed for: the importance of nucleus organisation in the building business, as explained on page 132. This organisation includes labour which is classed as direct-cost from the costing point of view. The constant-average-direct-costs generalisation is therefore misleading when one considers the immediate effects on a business of fluctuations in its activity, or if one is to understand the drives which pressure an individual business in the market, even keeping to the present plane of generality.[14]

As we have seen, to hold, and develop from, its market position, a building firm must keep its nucleus organisation and we may suppose it reasonable to assume that it does this at least over the normal range of fluctuations in its output. It follows that the cost of nucleus labour must be seen as a kind of additional overhead, increasing the weight of the fixed costs which must be deducted from total receipts to get profits and, further, it will add its quota to the unavoidable amount which must be paid out in cash whatever the output.

It is strategically important that the building management will be conscious of the increased profits and cash gains which increases in output will tend to bring; and equally will it be aware of the drain on cash and the risk of disproportionate loss which falling activity will entail. This will be so, even when allowance is made for the business doing what it can to minimise costs and charges by using nucleus labour as flexibly as possible to make maximum economy in other labour, and with rising output, lessen the effects of taking on labour which is not habituated to it (such causes of rising direct costs themselves not being allowed for in the simple model under discussion).

This report does not discuss in any detail the question of the diversity of activity which individual firms will experience, as one gets hit or another gains by some chance outside itself or by some opportunity which is taken or not taken. Looking at the industry's economics in the large, we remember that in all the individual diversity there is a common movement of the industry due to the importance of the general market environment, and common influences at work even in local or particular markets. To use a Manchester phrase, 'when it's one o'clock for me, it's one o'clock for everyone else'. Typically, when one business is finding the market slack or is pressed with new work on offer, its competitors are more than likely to be in the same position. This means that in the typical case of actually rising outputs, our 'constant average direct costs', which is the static tendency, will dynamically be translated into rising levels of direct costs (with a tendency for other costs to rise as well, as a whole market experiences the same pressure on resources).

But the pressure for increased output will remain at the individual business level; it will still be true that cash flows will be higher and profits more buoyant if output is increased, and that any losses of profits due to falls in its activity will be matched by increased outflow of cash. The organisation of the general building market will mean that any one job will regularly be offered to a number of firms, whether in formal tender or not; and in this industry two other factors must be remembered. First, there is the regular experience of markets, and sections of markets, which turn down, and especially after periods of sharply rising demand. Sharp reversals are commonplace for capital-goods industries in ordinary recessions; they have been no less typical in the 'stops' which are part of the short-term management of the economy, and building has often been specially affected as an instrument as well as a subject of such policies. The further ahead a builder looks in his plans, the less certain he must be that there will not be a shortage of work. Second, as we have seen, the building firm has peculiar problems of balancing its activity among a diversity of projects, and there will be a varying desirableness for it of particular jobs which will have much to do with its balance of work and little with the general situation, all businesses wanting work as they look far enough ahead, and in the nearer future being rather short of the kind of works which would better balance their affairs.

In the shorter-term balance, the starts on bigger jobs may have their own attractions and difficulties; far enough ahead some 'lining' of the large jobs (bigger and large being relative matters) will be wanted as a foundation of the programme yet to be established. Even if current trade be high, one can then understand the keen competition which a builder will offer for a suitable large job which comes over his planning horizon. Within the relevant size scale, the minor jobs offered at varying periods ahead and the smaller jobs more or less available at all times will especially attract the competition of those who 'can do with them'; the balance of work assumed in simple cost generalisations thus having to be striven for by practical businesses. The balance of their foreseeable work was a matter to which the seminar's builders paid careful attention. As an example relevant to what we have just been discussing, we may mention one who described his firm's regular 'look-ahead' analysis three months before the end of major contracts in hand so as to know whether to 'go' next for a 'brick' or a 'concrete' tender.

The market consequences which are here foreshadowed will concern us more later on. The point from the present sub-section is that the pressure for increased output, which one would expect in the abstract because of the general cost advantages of running full and the competitive structure of the industry, will be intensified in building markets where bids are so affected by the discrepancies in individual business situations, as managers strive to make consistent longer-run programmes out of individually discontinuous and highly diverse jobs.

### Effects of size of job

This is a subject where more research data would be needed to get beyond very broad generalities and assess the interconnecting, and separate, influences on costs of size of job, size of output, and the organised scale of a business. We go into it now only so far as seems helpful to other sections, notably because of some interesting implications, for the maintenance of market position and the further development of a building business, of the relative attractions to it of jobs of different sizes, as apart from the fact that bigger jobs may be offered further in advance of the start of work.

Of course, there are interrelations between job-size, output and scale of business — some individual jobs are so large that they are larger than the total output of a relatively small firm or, more realistically, larger than the proportion of projected output which a firm is prepared to have in one basket, and so large that some firms will not have the organisation to service them; and the other side of that coin is that some businesses will be too small for a customer to let them have works above a certain size. The larger jobs, again, include some of the most complicated ones, e.g. hospital complexes, and will involve higher costs in themselves than typical smaller jobs. But, by and large, it appears that costs seem likely to fall with larger jobs of the same general class, provided that a firm is organised or can readily extend to cope with them. The larger the job of a given kind, the more repetition of operations there tends to be: for example, in a large building, there may be many identical concrete columns to be shuttered, many identical doors to be made and hung in identical frames. In building as in other industries with very low runs of individual products, the reduction of costs through the 'learning factor' may produce substantial savings in labour costs with larger projects. It is easier to keep gangs continuously employed than if they have to move between smaller jobs, and the saving in dead time must be added to the cost benefits of more continuous employment as a team. There will also be some saving on materials with larger-scale buying or handling.

On top of savings in direct costs, there will also tend to be savings in management overheads, for the job and for the business as a whole. Less supervision will be needed where men work more continually at the same job and on the one site. Small jobs will require part-time attention from managers whose skills may be more efficiently concentrated on larger jobs. On the other hand, the realised gains from the larger job may not belong simply to its size but may result from a natural and extra degree of attention just because it bulks so large in the firm's output, and so visible gains may to some extent have less visible management costs to offset them. This brings up another, but related point: as between jobs of very different sizes, there may be a 'quantum jump' in management costs in so far as the complexities of larger jobs may call for a different, more highly trained and paid, class of site management altogether (although there may still be economies from such managers working on still larger jobs). Even on the direct-cost side, more 'amenities' may have to be provided on larger jobs, quite apart from the fact that more may be expected on the largest jobs, the province of the biggest businesses where the scale of amenities may help to compensate for increased remoteness of central management. This, in turn, has a related point – that there may be greater risk of, and greater managerial costs in preventing, friction among and with labour at the really large-project sites.

On balance, however, the generalisation stands that there will be gains to the individual firm from increasing size of job, even though it may expect more gains, from experience of smaller-scale work, than may actually be realised. This then is another factor increasing the direct attractiveness of the larger jobs – and where 'larger' begins of course depends on the size scale of a firm at present. There is a further point, that its larger jobs bring it more prominently into its market as a firm to which relatively large responsibility has been given. When assessing market consequences of these factors, we need to remember one feature of the industry which makes it possible to take on larger jobs as occasion serves in a more gradual fashion; this is the possibility of putting work out on sub-contracts, so that a business extending in this way need only gradually take the full strain of carrying out increasing proportions of such jobs.

At the same time, when we look at the other end of the size scale of jobs taken on by a single firm, the fact that its small works will tend to cost more in proportion to size than larger works of the same kind does not mean that they will be proportionately less attractive, so prices quoted will not necessarily offset all the apparent, or suspected, cost disadvantages. For the smallest jobs, much evidence was given to the seminar that their efficient running was a management headache, and in some cases there was a clear feeling that they did not justify the bother in direct profits. (This was so even though at or beyond a medium size of firm, smaller jobs in general were organised in 'small works' departments.) But, on the credit side, there is the balancing role which smaller works peculiarly can play in the general programme of a business. Moreover, nearly always, a special justification was adduced in market conditions: small works are more frequently offered by individual customers than are large, so that a wide circle of potential clients may have goodwill towards the builder when they have larger jobs to offer; and small works are physically widespread enough to act as a continuing and general advertisement. For the new firm starting small, where entry is easiest, of course, small jobs must be its bread and butter, and this may be seen as the start of the competitive chain in which the smaller works which a builder of any size feels he has to keep, are yet, or seem to be, relatively less profitable to him, and so on all the way up the size scale.

Increasingly, we have strayed from costs, strictly regarded, to considerations of markets and of firms' growth and development in their markets. The question of the market will be more conveniently resumed in the next section, but we may turn more directly now to the question of growth via a consideration of economies arising from the scale of business.

### Costs and size of business

The element of current costs, because of their practical importance, links an abstract model of short-run cost/output relationships with situations of direct practical interst, such as prices and profit and loss. The long-run model (which relates costs to size on the basis that, at any point on the size scale, costs will be those applicable to a business which is completely organised to run at that scale of operations) is more removed from reality, except in the case of whole business units set up *de novo*. True, a businessman looks to the sort of factors which underlie such a model, when he plans growth and adds further plant, etc. to what he has already, but he will be heavily aware of constraints not featured in the model and his planned growth will have to be seen in a context, not of stationary perfection but of growth itself.

What one can say, with such a long-run model in mind, is that one would not expect the cost aspect to be a deterrent to the growth of a building firm; that a business which is pressing at, or going beyond, the upper limits of the short-run range of output for which it is organised will find that it pays to grow to a larger scale and a new output range; further, that one would expect a business's average costs per unit actually to be lower when fully reorganised to cope with a larger norm of output (of the same type, understood) than when at a lower norm. But in building, in particular, it seems of doubtful value to go beyond this and think of ideal costs in the abstract as effectively settling long-run tendencies of prices. As already explained (note 8), in sectors where this industry is very easy to enter, the competitive level of prices is not hoisted to such a cost floor. In specialised market sectors and those where really large firms predominate, putting on one side the competition which will push up from below, the cross-entry competition of established firms may similarly be more effective. There is also the point that, practically, the growth which is involved in scale takes time, and a business which has *grown* to a given size may well be striving to grow further, so that its market impact may be greater than might be expected from a calculation of what its costs could be if it remained at that size.

The seminar's agenda paper took us and the businessmen into personal attitudes to growth as a start in understanding actual development. It was clear that none of the small or medium-sized firms that were interviewed was conscious of being at a disadvantage compared with larger firms met in actual competition or generally. One or two said that they did not wish to grow further – but in each case this was connected with keeping family financial control and direct family management, rather than with any expectation of diseconomies of growth. Equally, no large firm expressed regret at being 'too large', although it was recognised that size may entail changes in the system of management and perhaps in the type of jobs done.

These general views are consistent with the fact that firms of very different sizes do continue to exist in building. The predominant factor may well be the benefits of close personal management, so that over some size ranges in the shifting world of actual building, smaller businesses may make up for static cost disadvantages and have positive advantages which larger businesses have to counteract with more expensive organisation, offsetting any gains in pure production costs. Another important factor, however, is the way that building works may divide into sectors which, perhaps, specially suit firms of particular ranges of size; and the smallest firms, for example, may dominate certain sectors, the thrust of their competition carving out these sectors from the general market.

Repairs and maintenance, and small works, in so far as these are a separable class of activity, seem to be very much a field for smaller businesses. The larger firms doing such work seem to organise it almost as a quite independent business, involving as it does, close personal attention by management to the detail of the work, to clients' idiosyncrasies and to the supervision of labour. Much the same probably applies to the scattered building of a few houses at a time, an activity which seems specially associated with the smaller local builder. It is on larger sites and larger regular flows of work of the same kind that the organisation of a large firm can come into play.

In view of the tendency to correlation between job size and firm size, there will be some spillover from the economies of size of individual jobs, already discussed, into economies of scale to a business. We have also seen how the larger kinds of jobs available to a business make natural focus-points for any policy of growth. A separate way in which a business may gain from size arises through the numbers of jobs it may have on the go at the same time, because of the greater ease of scheduling work so as to smooth out the different and varying demands for labour skills and for other resources at successive stages of individual jobs. The extent of labour economies of this kind will, however, be limited by the localisation of building to the area in which a common labour force may be raised and deployed. Beyond this, scheduling may gain from the use of pools of mobile equipment and teams of specialists, as from the use of central management facilities, but the division of responsibility between central management and local operation is likely to add to management costs. It is understandable how the localisation of site activity makes the regional and area organisations crucial levels in the management of national-scale businesses.

By and large, indeed, building with its very diversified market and localisation of activity seems pre-eminently an industry which must offer room for many different kinds and sizes of firms. Despite what has been said of the pressures of short-run costs making for running as full as possible, and therefore pushing towards the overall growth of a business, actual growth can well be held in check by effective competition from other firms also bent on running full. Nor can growth occur too rapidly. There is the purely financial aspect. Because of the almost automatic extension of working capital through trade credit from suppliers and the fairly continuous repayment of a large part of outlays on account, plus the general credit standing of a growing business with its bank, etc., growth itself may be thought to be relatively easy, as well as tempting, having regard to the risks and difficulties of a building business. But the firm which grows rapidly by using external finance for current activities may prove to be over-extended and not only susceptible to a financial squeeze but also vulnerable to the ordinary accidents of its life,

which might be weathered with greater short-run financial independence.[15] Again, there is the need to maintain balance between the various
sectors of a business, and it is difficult to maintain balance in a rapid
expansion of output. On the other hand, it is easier to maintain a balance
of work with some rate of growth than with none, and the smaller the
business the greater the effect of this factor. If imbalance looms, for
whatever reason, it may be corrected by successful tendering for further
work of the right kind and at the right time; and a firm which does this
will tend to continue growing as the effort to provide fuller employment
in one department tends to create the need to take on extra men at later
stages.

There are other patterns of growth which are more matters of taking
advantage of idiosyncratic opportunities for growth than anything
systematically related to the general schemata of business theory; for
instance, to state an obvious case, a business discovering that it is
particularly successful in one type of construction may channel most of its
expansion into this field, and change its 'balance' accordingly. A successful
company may simply have surplus income which it uses to enter a new
market. A company which has grown already for a long enough period
may have built-in drives for growth and tend not to debate its desirability.
One instance which came up in the seminar showed an influence of this
kind stemming from a management training programme which, inevitably,
needed a larger intake than could be matched by the higher echelon of the
current establishment of responsible career jobs; on the one hand, the
business looked grudgingly on the prospect that a number of the better
men it had recruited should pass on to competitors; on the other hand,
trainees got down to their work the more keenly the more they felt they
could rely on actual trends of growth; this was felt to be a major factor
making growth a business objective in its own right.

So long, however, as growth does not take place too fast for effective
control or for the balance of operations or for the availability of finance,
we return to the generalisation that the efficiency of a business should not
fall off when it has adapted itself to a larger scale of management and
operation, assuming that the firm is doing jobs which are suitable for its
scale. As a business grows, however, one must expect that a greater degree
of administrative organisation will involve management overheads rising by
comparison with other costs and one would expect that capital costs
would also rise in proportion to output, granted a tendency to heavier
investment in plant and equipment. In evolving an organisation which suits
the carrying out of larger contracts, a firm may handicap itself for jobs
which run at significantly smaller scales, in so far as the work may be

carried out without much benefit from any more elaborate provision set up for larger jobs, or as the personal management of smaller firms on such smaller projects may offset any advantages that do arise. The larger firm may then conclude that in terms of costs, for such and such a class of jobs, its 'overheads' are too high, whether these are in the form of head-office services or of site overheads. The seminar had such experience reported to it, special reasons being given for carrying on with such lower-profit jobs.

This still leaves open the question of the effect of costing-systems in allocating too heavy a proportion of overheads at the smaller-contract end of the range. There is a parallel point *vis-à-vis* the smaller business: taking on relatively large contracts on a one-at-a-time basis, it may well be possible to run them relatively cheaply compared with the costs of the organisation which the business would have to set up if it handled contracts of such a size as a regular affair of numbers of such jobs. Equally, there is the pure accountancy point that proper allocation of overheads may not matter for a small proportion of total output, but must be right if the proportion grows sufficiently. In any case, the point remains that businesses who may specialise on contracts which are attractive as more isolated ventures to others will have to meet a correspondingly sharp competition.

When discussing growth, the importance of site management was stressed throughout our inquiry. The smaller firm may be able to be more flexible and its principals may be able to spend enough time on the sites personally to counteract any weaknesses in subordinate management (or can do very well with lower-paid, lower-calibre there). On the other hand, larger firms can probably afford to get and hold better-quality managers (and equally may need them at subordinate levels in order to get maximum benefit from a more distant kind of central management). In any case, however, a firm contemplating growth will see the availability of site managers of the right quality as essential if it is to take on more jobs, and at the national level this factor may be a real bottleneck not only for growth of individual businesses but also for any reorganisation of the industry to take advantage of changing technology. A number of our witnesses made it clear that they could not finalise a tender until they knew which particular site agent would be allocated to the job, because the event would make a substantial difference to costs. Even if all site managers were equally efficient, there was still the danger of having to use, say, a concrete specialist on a brickwork job; so that, as one witness put it, either on-costs or prime costs might go up, so that one would 'need £6000 (in profits) for a £4000 man'. Another firm, because of the effect of efficiency at the foreman level, tried to keep its labour in teams, each headed by a trades foreman, which would move from job to job together. Because the adverse effects of a job 'going wrong' may be more powerful as a negative factor than the positive gain in profits of a job which is going well, we found examples of good site managers being moved around as trouble-shooters, no matter where plans may have allocated them.

Site managers down to the foreman level are perhaps the most important part of the nucleus which a firm will want to keep in being whatever the temporary trade conditions, a core which cannot be added to quickly or easily replenished if it declines. Around them, largely, the business will decide its strategy and with them it will carry out its tactics as it moves continuously from present jobs to future through its quotations and tenders. Coming back once more to a general view of long-term costs, it is this stability at the centre, giving a business its continuity, amidst all the pressures for growth and with all the reasons for orderly growth, which enables it to take its present costs as a reasonable basis for estimates of future costs; with all the chances and flux of business life it may hope, with continued effort, to do as well; and with growth it may do better.

### The question of business idiosyncracy and economic generalisation

The scope for individuality in the building firm, for differences in the development and in the internal organisation of businesses, is the other side of the openness of the industry to competition through the combined effect of factors which have been discussed already — e.g. the diversity of the market, the general lack of strong economies or diseconomies of scale of firm, the feasibility of sub-contracts, the organisational flexibility generally, and, indeed, the importance of the managerial function in itself. Since a report of the present kind on this particular industry necessarily involves generalising about what is in actuality so individual a phenomenon, it seems that it should not burke the disquiet which people with practical knowledge of actual businesses may feel at this kind of abstraction.

The point is that, although any discussion of the economics of the building firm must (as recognised at the very beginning of this section) start from its basic idiosyncracy of character, the idea of 'character' is as much concerned with stable traits in abstract industrial application as it is in application to human personality. A business's location, its previous history and the policy of its management, and the financial resources it deploys, will decide the precise character which the business has in terms of where it is *aimed* in the market. Activities will thus be centred and this will affect expected performance in particular operations, both in jobs which are in the main line of the business and in the other jobs which are fitted into its programmes. These latter jobs will not suit it so well as they suit other firms to which they are more 'main line', and we should expect cost differences to follow those of market specialisation. We may add a recognition of systematic differences in the prices of factors of production (for example, differences in labour costs due to differences in catchment areas). Without going into more debatable questions concerning normal, long-run differences in operational performance which can arise purely from reasons internal to the firm, we should expect as *normal* quite marked differences in the costs at which individual businesses would carry out comparable building operations, even if 'costs' were fully standardised.[16]

Beyond such normal, persistent differences, actual costs will have substantial interfirm variances, shorter term, due to the fluctuating effects of weather and site conditions, to short-period changes in levels of activity, and the chance variations which will affect performance on any actual job, as well as differences in sheer 'efficiency' which must be expected at any one time. These 'random' cost differences raise no problem for any theory of business tendencies, though a world in which they occur may require a different kind of organisation, and therefore different cost structures, than would be developed in a world which was free from such uncertainties.

So far as normal analysis of long-run tendencies is concerned, general economics need not be concerned with every variation to be found within a competitive industry. It rather considers the general framework through which competition acts and the directions of tendency under the influence of particular forces; for this purpose one may abstract from stable, persistent, 'characteristic' differences between one business and another, *except* where they become relevant as correlated with a difference in *kinds of response* to changing economic circumstances.[17] This will be remembered in the discussion of market behaviour to which we now turn. For the moment, let it be stressed that any such generalising in terms of regularities of behaviour should not be seen as presuming uniformity of individual circumstances or position. The real diversity of businesses has to be read back into general theory when it is applied to practical circumstances and actual individual firms. In such practical use, theoretical generalisations may be no more than bench-tools for the roughing-out of an approach to the problem in hand, but without them, practical problems may lack the shaping-up which is necessary for solutions to be found.

THE PRICING OF BUILDING WORKS: COMPETITIVE TENDERS
MARKET SECTORS IN BUILDING

For the purpose of theorizing about the prices of building works, one may distinguish three major sectors of the general building market, each of which has its special features – or four sectors, if we separate off repairs and maintenance as a rather special case. Two sectors include works initiated by the purchasers of the buildings concerned, and are distinguished one from the other by the way in which prices are settled; the first, where the price for a particular job is negotiated between customer and a chosen builder, 'negotiated' contracts; the second, where the price is settled by competitive tender to customer's specification, 'competitive tenders' which may be (a) open to all comers, reached by some form of advertisement, 'open' tenders, or (b) open only to invited builders, 'selective' tenders. The third sector consists of the 'speculative' works where the builder has the initiative, controlling the design specification and practical quality and quoting price at whatever level he thinks appropriate as he offers to the market of potential customers what are 'his' products, produced as his own speculation and at his own risk, in so far as all the planning and a good deal of construction will ordinarily take place in advance of sales.

The fourth sector, of repairs and maintenance works, is perhaps too often discussed, and criticised, as if its performance can be judged by the same criteria as new works. Although there may be nothing special about the contractual arrangements for them as compared with those of the first two classes of new works, there seem to be good organisational grounds for their separate analysis, e.g. (i) the relative smallness, and yet the range of size and type even so, of individual works of this class, which generally impose constraints both on customer and on builder in their planning and execution; in this sense, 'r. and m.' works seem necessarily to be more primitive organisationally than new works, depending more on individual skills and being less facilitated by investment in preliminary organisation and capital equipment, (ii) the extent to which such works are especially open to competition from smaller businesses, partly in consequence of (i), and the extent to which their prices are subject to only a weak long-run cost floor (see remarks about the effects of hopeful assessment of long-run prospects wherever entry is particularly 'easy', p. 129), (iii) the extent – no doubt largely in consequence of the preceding two factors – to which the departments of larger businesses carrying out such works are justified, at least partly, by reason of benefits to the business as a whole, rather than their direct profitability (see p. 140).

We return to market sectors other than repairs and maintenance, in order to discuss organisational aspects which may similarly call for distinctive analysis. The possibility of adjusting specifications to facilitate carrying out the works, and also the possibility of giving scope for the builder's initiative in timely collaboration to explore and meet special needs of the customer, were reasons why the seminar's witnesses from larger businesses liked the 'package deals' which are a special kind of negotiated contract; even medium-sized businesses expressed wishes that the general building market were organised more in terms of such contracts, criticising the restrictiveness of tender contracts from the same point of view. Apart from this factor, i.e. given the specifications, probably the major economic point of distinction between negotiated and tender contracts is the relative openness to uncertainty and other short-term influences in the case of tenders, the quoting builders working more in the dark and more at arm's length from the customer. This point is of some practical significance in view of the important kinds of work which are characteristically put out to tender, and will have its bearing on the low level of profit margins which, it will be suggested, competition under the tender system favours.

As between open· and selective tenders, discussion in the seminar was chiefly concerned with the latter. Open tenders were generally disliked by our witnesses, most of whom would go in only for selective tenders, where bids were invited from known firms and each therefore 'knew the competition'; an important aspect of this was the indication thereby given of the standard of quality to be expected on the particular job; but they could also judge the extent to which there might be the risk of a firm bidding on the basis of general desperation as distinct from a bid sharpened by special reasons to have the particular contract in question rather than other work currently on offer.[18] (It may be said that the customer may also have an interest in avoiding placing work with 'desperate' firms, but one must realise the difficulties which may stand in the way of customers accepting any other than the lowest tender in cases where open tenders are adopted.) Of course, had the seminar's witnesses been from new businesses, aggressive for growth for whatever reason, we might have heard more about open tenders as a way of breaking into 'charmed circles', even though open tenders are not so characteristic of the post-war building market as are selective tenders.

The economics of speculative building has to start with some sort of general market analysis, even in the simplest models, because such work differs from both negotiated contracts and tender contracts in that the products are not pre-ordered by individual customers but have to be offered ready-made to a general market in a way which is not true for those other kinds of works.[19] Another theoretical aspect of speculative building is that the adjustment of specifications to make the most of the market must be seen as involving shifts in both demand and cost functions.

The complete operational freedom of speculative building had led to one of the seminar's builders concentrating upon housing for which he had developed limited but attractive standard designs, which he put up only on sites which would take at least minimum numbers from the point of view of economy of construction, selling, etc. With this specialisation, he had also made special savings as a result of methods of control of buying and the organisation of the actual delivery of the standard supplies and components designed into his house. The business had grown considerably but further growth would be more difficult (being limited by the availability of sites within its working area, etc.). The owner was trying to maintain growth by using the cost advantages of his methods as the basis for negotiated contracts from public authorities whose needs were normally met by competitive tenders. But is there any permanent escape for an individual within a system? The business's special efficiencies might at the moment bring gains which at present were most easily available through him; the case, however, brought up the interesting possibility that, once the customer authorities had learnt how to specify and control the operational innovations in a general fashion, the extension of the market would be on the ordinary tender basis; in assessing the future, the benefits from this business's special experience, exploited under the influence of its owner's views of reasonable profits in negotiated contracts, might well come to seem outweighed by the chances in competitive tenders from others, whose own normal market (via tenders) this firm would temporarily have cut into.

### Relationship between sectional markets and general theory

Ideally, any general analysis of pricing in building needs to be grounded in separate and specialised analyses of the basic sectors whose distinctive characteristics have been discussed, not least because of the interrelationships which must arise between them as individual firms exercise their choices between different kinds of works in the overlapping competition which characterises the industry. Since the seminar chose to concentrate on competitive tenders, any more general view of building prices will be limited somewhat by what can be seen from this vantage point. Nevertheless, at the most general level, there will be common features in the analysis of prices no matter what sector of the building market is considered; and it is these common features which would give a distinctive character to the analysis of the pricing of building works, in any general model, as compared and contrasted with the kind of manufacturing industry usually considered in economic theory. We shall not now go on to elaborate such a general model since it is inappropriate for the present report; but the features which would distinguish it have already been mentioned under 'Economic analysis' as special characteristics of the industry as a whole, and in the previous section as organisational aspects of the individual firm. Common to both sectoral and general analyses would be the use of costings to arrive at competitive quotations, which is considered as part of the economics of tendering *per se* below, and the attractions of taking on any particular work of any kind would emerge from the assessment of its role in the maintenance and development of the overall balance of the business, discussed in the previous section and again, operationally, in the latter part of this section. First, however, we take a general view of the competitive tender system, in some amplification of what has already been said about it.

## SUMMARY VIEW OF COMPETITIVE TENDERS

In essence, the procedure for a contract for new works let by tender is: the customer describes in detail the job he offers, typically with the use of architectural drawings and a bill of quantities which measures the various elements of the building in a standard way; then, individual builders who wish to compete for the job collect all other information from architect, suppliers, sub-contractors, visits to the actual site, etc.; each builder then 'prices up' the work, preparing the detailed estimates, 'costings' as we shall call them, on the basis of which, after any detailed readjustments and with additions for overheads and profit, he will go into tender. The details of the 'prices' on the completed bill of quantities, returned with the bid, have separate status in so far as both client and builder will use them to reckon allowances for changes in design, etc. at any later stage in the work (and more will be said about these ingredient-prices in due course, for there are some nice points about their theoretical position); finally, the individual bids having gone in, the basic principle of the competitive tender system, the customer having settled what he wants, is that the contract shall be awarded to the lowest bidder.

There is no difference in principle, nor therefore in economic theory, as between open and selective tenders. As was noted above, where customers are obliged – or choose – to have *open* tenders, it is usually difficult not to accept the lowest tender, unless for some glaringly obvious reason, even if there be the disparities in quality of performance feared by the seminar's builders (see p. 148). Now, in the case of *selective* tenders, with which the seminar was chiefly concerned, to take the lowest bid is especially reasonable: a prime consideration is that the competing firms will have been selected by the customer and his advisers as being acceptable builders anyway; further, as will be clear from what has been said in the preceding section about the influence of his currently known balance of work on the individual builder, and as will be seen in other detail below, businesses are affected by all sorts of considerations of advantage to them when deciding their bids, and the resulting *normal* spread of prices is the basis on which the customer may fairly choose to his best advantage, which is why after all the work is put out to tender.[20] Any theoretical model of the tendering system must therefore presume what will usually be the case, that the lowest bid for any work becomes the effective price for it, and that price will then take its place in the data from which competitors in *other* contracts will form their ideas of the trends of the market within which they are bidding.

A general point which interests an economist is, indeed, how the tender system establishes a kind of market system for new building works despite the three, as it might be thought powerful, obstacles which are inherent in the industry, viz. the idiosyncratic diversity of individual building works, the relatively infrequent need for such works by most private customers, including businesses, whose demand is most likely to be derived from considerations of the demand for final industry products, and finally, the great importance of the demands of public authorities, which may be influenced by budgetary policy at the social level but only remotely by commercial factors. As was suggested in the previous section, the working level of the market system can be seen as the individual building operations which can be specified, measured and costed; any abstract models must run in terms of whole-building products which are standardly synthesized from such elements. Whilst, however, the theory of long-run tendencies can as well run in terms of normal costs in building as in any other manufacturing industry, it is probably even more necessary to allow for short-run deviations because the building market, at least so far as concerns the important sector where works are let by tender, is organised so as to give such considerable scope for short-term influences. And even less in the case of building than in other industries should one assume that actual prices in such an important sector need to cover all the economic costs involved in working for that sector. All this is best seen in terms of the process by which the individual firm establishes its bid for some particular new-work contract.

THE MAKING OF A BID

A builder may tender for a job for other reasons than that he wants the contract. In particular:

(i) He may have been asked to tender by a client or architect who frequently has work which he would like the chance of doing, and not to quote may reduce his chances of being asked again.

(ii) He may want to check the competitiveness of his costs and prices in the current state of the market for what is within his ordinary range of work.

(iii) He may want to keep his estimating department's hand in with regard to such a job.

(iv) He may be testing what would be a new market for him to get some idea how competitive he might be if he went for that kind of work.

If a particular job is not wanted, then 'highish' prices may be put in, especially if the client be not of the 'regular' kind mentioned in (i) above, and if the builder would be prepared to do the work if it were unusually remunerative. More casual clients can of course be directly refused fairly easily and, in general, the seminar's witnesses thought it preferable not to tender but to explain the reason and try to keep goodwill, rather than to put in a bid which would be outside their normal range of price for that class of work in serious tender; in no case apparently are people inclined to quote a very high price, one which would be 'unrealistic'.

As a general matter, and within the limits of 'realistic' bids, however, a builder can pursue all the objectives listed above. For example, experienced builders evidently think they have enough knowledge of what is happening to tender prices to be reasonably sure of losing a contract in case (i), without irritating possible future clients, or giving them, and, possibly others, a wrong idea of their expectations about the prices they should get for their work. The other objectives fall more easily into place in the usual run of tender pricing. The important point here is that, although builders can get work only by tendering for particular jobs, they have to think in terms rather of getting a sufficient proportion of the jobs of any particular kind which come their way, as a class. There is no way of being sure of a particular job, except by quoting at so low a level that any builder who thus made sure of his programme in terms of particular contracts with only those bids would normally be equally certain of making a loss. And, within the range of 'reasonable' prices, however low one goes for a given job, someone may well go lower and even a small margin may get the contract, or, where bids are very close together, someone else may be preferred even if one is lowest.

Typically then, a builder must quote for a number of contracts on the chance that he will get a sufficient proportion of them to give him the stream of work which he needs to keep his business growing. Among our witnesses, the larger companies in fact reckoned to succeed in about 15 per cent of all the tenders they submitted, and the family firms generally claimed a 20 or 30 per cent success rate (but often higher for the smaller jobs). The jobbing builder reckoned that he was successful with 50 per cent of his bids. These rates are approximate, as it was unclear in some cases whether the number of tenders included those to test a new market, or to check competition, or to stay on a list of selected competitors, such contemporary circumstances being difficult to isolate when looking at remembered overall figures. These special considerations may perhaps affect medium to larger firms more than others; and the differences between the figures probably reflect the overhead incidence of the sheer cost of making tenders, already referred to, which will bear more heavily on the organisation of the smaller business.

The need to balance his activity by getting this desired stream of work out of successions of overlapping contracts, means that it will be normal for a builder to be sufficiently regularly 'in' the parts of the market where he ordinarily works for him to keep checks on prices of the kind mentioned under (ii) above. If he gets 'out of line' he will tend to be shut out of a number of contracts and so be short of work, or offered more than is convenient so that he tends to be 'swamped'. The individual contract, then, has to be set inside a wider framework from the firm's point of view, and decisions on individual contracts will reflect 'policy' decisions regarding works of that class and the kind of work in general. From the economist's point of view, this probabilistic approach to the market must be a distinctive feature of theory of the building industry: to summarise, the builder must be seen, it is suggested, not so much as bidding for this or that contract, but as quoting prices which will give him some regular chance of contracts of that kind. The details of what enters into the weighing of the attractions of such and such a contract which will sway the eventual bid will be further considered after more has been said about the preliminary details which have to be settled first.

### Pricing the bill

It has already been explained that the preparation of a bid starts with 'pricing the bill' (of quantities) supplied by the client, and then the final offer is obtained by adding to whatever total emerges from such details a further sum for overheads and profit. So far as getting the tender is concerned, the final, overall total is the effective 'price' bid for the work;

but the details of the individual 'prices' on the bill have, as already said, the practical significance that both parties will use them for evaluating differences between the actual work, as the client settles it in practice, and the specifications of the tender. There seemed to be differing reactions to this fact as between the smaller and the larger businesses covered by our inquiry; but in both cases there was a strategic element in the final decision about some prices at all events.

In particular, the business specialising in reconstructions (and so dealing for the most part with relatively small clients) was in a market where it had not only to look at the competitiveness of its quotation in relation to the standard of quality required by the client, but also to regard as normal any variations which went far from the plans on which the quotation was made. In this market, apparently, the details of basic pricing as distinct from details of specification are not gone into so thoroughly in the estimates as in tenders using ordinary b.o.q.'s, and the client pays for his nuisance value; in fact, our particular business found that it could rely on increases to cover such variation to add substantially to the *a priori* profitability of its reconstruction works and so could quote more keenly where it expected such changes of intention.

Builders from larger businesses, however, were more worried about adverse effects of changes in specification, probably because, on the tenders for new work which predominate with them, it would not be so possible to get retrospective compensation. Thus, for example, a given job might, as it went to tender, include a good deal of asphalt work; a builder, who might, indeed, have gone for the contract to some extent because that work was there, would in any case price and quote on the basis of the efficient carrying out of the quantity named in the bill; after the contract was awarded, the client might have a change of plan, greatly reduce the amount of asphalt (possibly replacing it with work which the successful builder might not be able to do so readily at that particular time), and leave the builder stuck with the price level which would have paid him only if he had done the original work. One would expect that there would be some tendency for builders to try to guess where such changes are especially vexatious, so that normal prices would cover them; but such uncertainties must also mean larger risks in tendering and our larger builders clearly thought that it was improbable that, over the long run, prices would repay any major messing about with specifications by clients.

Both examples bring out the point that there may be considerable finesse in the making of detailed prices inserted on the bill, so that there would be room for more inquiry here and the upshot could affect the details of the theoretical pricing model. But for a first approach, one may stress the undoubtedly more important adjustments which are made in the addition for overheads and profit, discussed later. There remains the point that the formal separation of the priced elements does mark an important division of building costs, in so far as the entities measured correspond to what the economist or ordinary accountant knows as prime costs, those of materials and labour; but the separation is illusory so far as concerns the enonomic significance of the individual prices.[21]

We have previously made the essential point in all this, that the 'prices' of tenders are not 'costs',[22] but 'costings';[23] this distinction is important in all theoretical economic work which takes off from actual procedures, and especially important in building; one can be misled by the fact that costings use accounting information and are grouped under similar headings as those which economists, and accountants, would use for categories of costs, properly calculated. On pp. 129–30 we have similarly made the points that the organisation of the building industry means that it is competitive in terms of process stages, and that the building market may be conceived of as analysable into separate markets for the work done in the operational divisions of an entire building work, the latter being essentially too differentiated for the idea of *a* market to be directly applied, except in the most abstract model where all buildings might be assumed to be identical. This basic idea provides the rationale for the use of the costings of the b.o.q. in the whole making of tenders, through from the making of the detailed estimates and the addition of 'normal' margins for overheads and profit to the final adjustment of the whole price to meet special considerations affecting the particular tender.

Whereas the customer will take the *lowest* price in the tender, other things being equal, it is to the interest of the individual builder to set his prices so that he can generally get as *high* a price as is consistent with his tendering activity as a whole producing the required volume of work. Because no man can be entirely accurate in an uncertain world, this no doubt produces one of the pressures towards growth in large (and also efficient) businesses where tender contracts bulk large in their total work, as they try to price on the safe side. We return to this and other points about pricing *policy* in due course. Assuming, as we would, that an individual business has a consistent policy in each sector of the market which it finds distinctive for pricing purposes, the rationale of costings in a competitive market is that there should *normally* be regular relationships, *given* the prices of factors of production (e.g. its effective wage rates) and the working practice of the individual business, between the prime costs which it incurs at any stage in its operations and what it can get for any 'product' of that stage without losing an undue proportion of tenders to competitors (or substituting an undue proportion of sub-contracting for its own work).

Two further things need to be said in the march of the argument from *costs* to *costings* and the b.o.q. prices which embody these. The first is that businesses will in practice have different levels of prime costs for the same job-stage, depending on (i) the extent to which mechanisation and organisation have substituted capital equipment and other overheads for prime-cost labour, (ii) (given such considerations) their individual efficiences at that stage, (iii) sheer aberrations in accounting procedure and detail (so that, for example, one firm may not sort out so many prime-cost elements – leaving the balance to be covered by its overall margins – as another firm, perhaps more elaborately organised, identifies in its costs and costings).

The second point is that, as already explained, costings differ from costs precisely in that they anticipate market situations and are not calculated, as costs should be, solely with reference to operational expenses. If we are thinking of long-run tendencies of price, of normal prices in the theoretical sense, there is not so much special point in this, simply that a business will get an idea of what such and such an operation by it will be worth in its usual markets and 'cost it up' accordingly. But even this does lead to the interesting point (technically, economic rents being opportunity costs within a business) that, if the value in the market for the product of some individual or team exceeds what such people could earn from competitive employers, and so what they have to be paid, the firm may be able to identify an accounting surplus on the jobs in which it employs them. The seminar met this consideration, operating at the site-costs level, in a business which required those contracts to which it allocated its better site agents to earn more than others, charging figures which the management had decided (e.g. £6000) above the salaries concerned (e.g. £4000) as items in the costing of the contract.

The more important point for immediate purposes is that building is an industry where the flux of work in relation to capacities may produce strong movements of short-term prices (fluctuations around the long-run trends of 'normal' prices). This has to be allowed for in the firm's approach to the prices of building projects; the markets will vary in the short term for the individual kinds of building work which the various jobs will require in various proportions. For example, brickwork, excavation and foundations work, concrete work, interior finishing – all characteristically involve different kinds of labour and different doses of plant and equipment and will have their different market positions from time to time. In one area, for instance, the composition of demand for building work may shift, say, from brickwork to concreting; this we would expect to lead to prices on 'brick' contracts falling to lower levels in relation to strict costs than the levels of 'concrete' contracts. It would clearly be insensitive to try to allow for this by altering the margin for overheads, etc., when one would have to start to meet the market by allowing for the effect of the given different proportion of 'brick' work at the appropriate stage of the b.o.q. As our evidence showed, this is one of the factors which made our businesses anxious to keep their estimating departments' hands in on diverse kinds of work — it was recognised that their prices for details in the b.o.q. were intended to be affected by what was happening in these elementary sectors of the building market, so that short-term, actual costings depart the more sensitively from costs in any strict sense.[24]

As noted earlier, the seminar did not closely investigate actual costing in the pricing of b.o.q.'s. There would no doubt have been a rewarding exercise in this, as contributing to more detailed theory, but it would have to take place in builders' offices and use different research methods. There was enough discussion to establish that our businesses used broadly the same methods of measurement, etc. and of 'pricing up'. We may, then, leave present conclusions here as bringing out the main points to be borne in mind. There is, of course, some practical importance in the last point we have been discussing, that is, that some elements of profit may be hidden in the costing of the b.o.q., as explaining why unusually efficient businesses may continuously make more profit in their accounts than is budgeted for in their tenders (and so reported to any research inquiry as being the profit margin at which they aim).

MARGINS

The prime-cost items are thus included in the b.o.q., and to the total sum which is arrived at by the addition of these detailed items is added a further sum as allowance for overheads and profit. We have seen that there may well be an element of profit hidden away in particular prime-cost items where a firm is particularly efficient, but we are considering now the explicit overall margin added to prime costs. Each company had a slightly different method of calculating or including establishment charges, but often a single addition, covering both overheads and profits, was made to the estimate of direct site costs. It is often difficult to decide which overheads should be assigned to individual sites, and which should be shared equally between all developments. One speculative builder shared all design and development charges between all sites, on the grounds that development costs of one particular type of dwelling should not be charged to the site on which the type is first erected, because in the long run this type might or might not account for a major portion of the company's turnover. Development work of this kind was seen as a necessary part of the company's general overheads. Another firm recognised the relative efficiencies of site managers, by allocating overheads and contingency allowances to specific sites, in proportion to the firm's estimate of each manager's capacity to earn a profit.

Analytically we must be right to group together overheads and profit because both are equally subject to 'policy' decisions, and it is the size of the overall margin which is in effect determined by 'what the market will bear' in price. On any one job many organisational costs will be overhead, and it is a matter of policy how much should be charged to this one job. It is similarly a matter of policy which site manager should be employed on which job, and the site manager has an effect on *all* classes of cost: there is not only his own salary cost, but his efficiency in organisation will affect all other overhead site costs, and the demands which a contract makes on the care and attention of central management, as it will also affect the attained levels of cost for prime-cost labour and materials. Moreover, there is no hard line between profit and costs. It is always possible to divert profits into costs, in effect, by spending on things which make a manager's life quieter and more comfortable, or giving the labour force better facilities, at the expense of lower net profits for the company. Hence the concept which Andrews named 'plasticity of costs' and is known to the behavioural theorists as 'organisational slack'.

Thus it is the size of the gross profit margin rather than the net profit margin which is the operative entity from the point of view of policy, and the margin will be looked at as a whole as well as in its constituent parts by building firms. It is also the whole margin which is held down as it were by the ceiling level of price. Arriving at a price to quote is the ultimate end of all the preparations which go into a tender. At the last stage, the cost estimates, prepared as carefully as they may be, have to be 'adjudicated'. In adjudication the amount estimated by the estimating department is converted into a tender sum by the addition of a positive or negative margin. This operation is always treated as a function of top management and is never performed by the estimating department. It is always undertaken by the person or persons with the ultimate responsibility for tendering; in the smaller companies one man may shoulder this responsibility for all contracts, and in larger companies different persons may be responsible for different-sized contracts and, for large contracts, the board of directors may take the necessary decisions. All the businessmen interviewed were concerned, one way or another, with adjudication.

The purpose of adjudication is to arrive at the right price. The company's desire for work, which has already been taken into account when deciding whether to accept an invitation to tender, now has a price attached to it – a low margin may be added if the company really needs the contract. But the main factor, especially with the larger companies, is the 'market'. In spite of the one-off nature of the job, our witnesses had an idea of a market price which they had to meet – a price influenced by the intensity of competition, the state of industry in the region and the industry's opinion of the state of demand in the coming months. Several businessmen believed their companies had sufficient knowledge of market prices to estimate their chance of obtaining a particular contract. It was claimed for one of the larger companies that the addition of a 5 per cent profit margin would give it a 60 per cent chance of gaining a contract, and if the margin added were increased to 7½ per cent the chance would be reduced to 30 per cent. Examples were also given of the extremely fine margins which might decide the award of a contract.

Looking at the matter in the abstract, as we have said, a building firm may be seen operationally as a management team which has associated with it a nucleus of labour and equipment which it regularly employs and to which it adds by hiring other factors of production as the exigencies of the short-run situation demand. Its object will be to secure the most profitable use of this nucleus organisation. The ideal would be to organise a stream of contracts in sequence which would exactly employ its balanced organisation (with whatever other factors it was necessary to hire alongside them) but the further it looks ahead the more difficult and the more risky it may be to plan to do this – some slack is necessary in order to be able to readjust to the actualities as they develop.

It follows that, looking relatively far ahead when its order books are fairly wide open, a business will be more attracted by larger nucleus-oriented contracts than it would be by smaller contracts or by contracts which are biased from its organisational point of view. Additional reasons for going especially for these contracts are that they are likely to last for longer periods of time than other contracts, and are more likely to put and keep the firm in the eye of prospective clients of the kinds it wants to attract. It is also a help that larger contracts are normally announced further ahead relatively, for given starting dates, than smaller contracts. A general model must therefore see a business as trying to adopt a policy which will bring a certain stream of nucleus-oriented contracts.

Of course it does not follow that these will be the same for all firms, because firms will be of different sizes and organisations. But within any one size class and type there will be relatively keen competition for the larger plums, both because of the organisational importance of such jobs and also because to secure a larger proportion of these is a necessary condition for balanced growth within the size class. It was noticeable that some of our small and medium-sized firms, asked whether they would put the same margin of profit on different-sized jobs, replied that they would take a lower margin on larger contracts. And it was a witness in a very large size class who coined the aphorism 'You cannot compete with a group below you'.

To tender for too many of these contracts, however, will entail a risk of being overfull with such work and thus falling down on the very contracts on which the firm most wishes to succeed. In the changing and uncertain conditions of the building industry, with starting dates postponed (or speeded up) and completion periods lengthening (or shortening) there must be a certain amount of slack to be taken up by other, complementary, shorter-term contracts. Looking now only a short distance ahead, as the operational uncertainties of building crystallise out, a firm will see the prospect of being out of balance in the use of certain facilities. It will try to get such contracts, therefore, as will take up the slack of its nucleus organisation. It may therefore be quoting very keenly for contracts which are relatively unbalanced from its longer-run point of view so as, for example, to use the relative surplus which the phasing of contracts has caused among its nucleus bricklayers, or to keep its concreting team together.

There are other reasons for keen quotations and low margins. A firm may want to get in with an important customer. Or it may think that if it can get one contract then others will follow. Thus it may quote very low on the first building for a new university or civic centre. Partly, of course, there are prestige considerations if a firm can link its name with a famous development, but there is also a cost consideration: that the second and third contracts will cost the firm who wins the first very much less than a newcomer, because of the 'learning factor', since both management and labour will have the sort of experience which in practice leads to substantial savings through more routinised working in a given site area.

Given that tenders are normally awarded to the lowest bidder, given that there will always be some firms operating at a loss, given that all firms will be trying to balance their work load, it is clear that most firms most of the time will be under pressure to keep their margins down. This is true, but it does not necessarily follow that most firms earn very low profits. We must distinguish between the margin allowed *ex ante* and the profits earned *ex post*. Part of the importance of the nucleus-oriented contract is that such contracts will by definition be of the kind of work for which the firm tends to be especially organised and which it can do at lower cost. As we have seen, the firm bases its tender not on its own (in this case, slightly below-average) costs but on the market price for the different operations, and it is quite possible that it would pay the firm to reduce its explicit nominal allowance for profit in order to increase its chance of gaining subsequently the profits implicit in the listed prices/costings of the various components of the bill. The firm will, of course, know this.

Post-accounting would show that such contracts, even with a low apparent margin, will be at least as remunerative as others. Again, within any one size class of firms, larger contracts will tend to mean lower costs because managerial skills can be better deployed, and this is something which will show up *ex post* rather than something which can be quantified *ex ante*. On what for firms are their smaller ranges of contracts the opposite position will hold. Here, the costing position may well be that they allow for at least their customary nominal margin and even perhaps a higher one, but in one way or another typically small contracts at any size scale will tend to be relatively unprofitable from a post-accounting point of view. The firms in question will not be especially organised for jobs of these sizes and such jobs will be the focus of attention for firms of a still smaller scale. Connexions from a smaller past may provide an historical reason why firms carry on meeting this kind of demand, but they make current sense only when they help create goodwill for more preferred business, or fill in the gaps for balanced production.

SOME GENERAL CONCLUSIONS

The work with the seminar impressed us with the differences between the building industry and the normal run of manufacturing industry. Yet, because of the long-term pressure of work on the building industry, thoughts are turning towards applying more of manufacturing and engineering techniques to the industry. The ordinary manufacturing firm is necessarily committed to a considerable long-term productive organisation, and markets are so organised that typically firms often forsake standardised products whose specifications change only in a systematic fashion. With identified products and a regular clientele, the factor of goodwill reinforces the long-run outlook which the settled productive establishment itself tends to create. Prices tend to be affected mainly by longer-term considerations and hence reflect normal costs.

In building, the nearest approach to this is the speculative builder who determines the specifications for his own product. But the firms moving into industrialised building are meeting the same problems in their need to have much larger orders of a standard type than is usual even in municipal housebuilding, to justify the setting up of a factory. Generally in building, the variability of the product and the effect of localisation of activity must be to produce a less settled establishment within the firm. One might, therefore, in any free competition, expect more flexible pricing in the building industry than in manufacturing. The resulting uncertainty may enforce a lower level of investment in equipment and a lower degree of fixed organisation than the volume of work actually available would warrant in a manufacturing kind of industry.

The tendering system must lead to a variability of price unknown to manufacturing industry. A particular contract is for a unique good in a particular place in particular circumstances, and these conditions will be favourable or otherwise to particular firms. It is also put out to tender at a particular time, and again conditions for any one firm will be variable over time. Variability of prices is thus linked to the market organisation. Again, for similar reasons, one would expect a range of actual prices on any one contract. But all this takes place within a market context. Firms tendering for a contract have an awareness of how prices are moving on this sort of thing. Price in this sense of price in equilibrium market conditions may be purely theoretical, but awareness of it affects how tenderers behave on a particular contract. Any one tenderer, in turn, will have an idea of a range of prices he might put in on one contract, associated with a range of probability of getting the contract.

In this chapter we have been in effect discussing the mean price level of a firm for any particular type of job and seen that, in the tendering system, it will depend on the relationship between the size of job and the size of firm, on the state of its order book for the period for which the tender should be executed, on the qualitative nuclearity of the job for the firm, or its complementarity with other projects to be executed at the same time from the company's limited resources, etc. There is also the question of the dispersion of the firm's prices about their mean, and this would appear to depend on the efficiency of the estimating department, on the lack of ambiguity in the procedures by which various special allowances and contingencies are provided for, and on the refinement of feedback arrangements from previous jobs. But it also depends on the policy of the firm as to the frequency with which tenders are prepared. For efficient playing of the tender game (of chance) knowledge is required of the relation between one's own mean price and the market mean and also some idea of the market dispersion as well as one's own. The role of such information is vital in tendering and hence the importance of unsuccessful tenders as much as successful ones in providing this information.[25]

An advantage of the tender system is that it provides a market and a competitive market price. Negotiated prices and package deals, etc. are becoming more common and save the costs of many firms' waste tenders, but it must be remembered that they can be entered into with more confidence just because there is a 'market' price established independently under free competition, which provides a background check. It is possible, however, that sufficient information on prices could be obtained without the tendering system: perhaps the publishing of prices on public contracts and the quantity surveyor's knowledge of the prices on other contracts passing through his office would be an adequate substitute. But negotiated contracts and alternative techniques to tendering have not been examined in any detail.

Our sample was small, probably unrepresentative, and only a proportion of the firms' business was got in the way we chose to study. We cannot therefore draw more general conclusions from the evidence we obtained. Nor is it possible to sort out what is due to the nature of the building industry and what is due to the tendering system, which itself arises from the nature of the industry. But the 'organisation' (if we may use a neutral term) has severe disadvantages at a time when we look forward to a long period of continued pressure on the building industry. *Ex post* we may see that there is, and has been for some time, a shortage of capacity; but *ex ante* each firm will be plunged in uncertainty with a 'lumpy' flow of work and a low chance of getting any particular contract. There will therefore be some tendency for contract prices to be continually depressed to a low level in the short run. In the long run, for the capacity of the industry to be maintained, price levels must be such that prices will on the average cover costs at least for the intramarginal firms, and those costs must include the costs of competitive tendering and estimating. The costs which have to be covered include all those which arise from the short-term emphasis of a tender system — the costs of firms balancing their operations and having to prepare tenders for far more work than will normally come to them.

Competitive prices are ensured by the ease of entry and other organisational factors to which we have called attention; but, more than that, it is difficult to imagine a building industry in which at any given time, in normal long-run conditions, a considerable margin of the industry will not be working at low profits and a sizeable proportion of work will not be carried out at a loss. Of course some firms will be forced out, but others will be taking their place, so that the unprofitable fringe in total will remain in existence. In building, measures of profitability in relation to capital invested must be expected to be very variable between the many different types of firm and could be quite misleading. We have the impression that profitability in this industry may be on the low side for 'reorganisation' (say on the industrial basis which is sometimes urged) to take place without some outside help or stimulus.

APPENDIX 5.1
Agenda headings for meetings with businessmen
*Decision-making in the area of costing and pricing*

1 A general view of your business.
2 How far do you size up a proposition before you decide to do anything serious about it? (For example, before preparing estimates in the case of tenders, or inquiring about the land in the case of a speculative proposition.)
3 What elements do you take into detailed account when preparing (cost) estimates?
4 How are your (cost) estimates affected by the size of the job?
5 Would your (cost) estimates be lower, if your business were rather larger?
6 How do you decide what to quote in the case of a tender?
7 How do you decide your price in the case of speculative work?

(Note: In questions 6 and 7 we shall be interested in how far factors other than cost estimates may affect particular quotations/prices.)

8 How do you know whether you have made a profit on a particular job?
9 Is there any point not covered so far to which you would like to refer?
10 Within the framework of the matters discussed, what in your view are the major problems facing your firm?

# Notes

CHAPTER 1
1. Elizabeth Brunner, 'A Note on Potential Competition', *Journal of Industrial Economics*, July 1961.

CHAPTER 2
1. I have drawn mostly on P. W. S. Andrews, *Manufacturing Business* (Macmillan, 1949). But see also Andrews, chapter 4, 'Industrial Analysis in Economics', in *Oxford Studies in the Price Mechanism*, ed. T. Wilson and P. W. S. Andrews (Oxford: Clarendon Press, 1951); and Andrews, chapter 1, 'Competition in the Modern Economy', in *Competitive Aspects of Oil Operations*, ed. G. Sell (Institute of Petroleum, 1958).
2. P. W. S. Andrews and Elizabeth Brunner, *Capital Development in Steel*, a study of the United Steel Companies Ltd. (Blackwell, 1951).
3. See, especially, Andrews's proof of evidence in *Books are Different*, as account of the defence of the Net Book Agreement before the Restrictive Practices Court in 1962, edited by R. E. Barker and G. R. Davies (Macmillan, 1966). The earliest application of his theory in this field was 'Some Aspects of Competition in Retail Trade', *Oxford Economic Papers*, 1950. See also Part II of *Fair Trade* by P. W. S. Andrews and Frank A. Friday (Macmillan, 1960).

CHAPTER 3
1. Robert Triffin, *Monopolistic Competition and General Equilibrium Theory* (Cambridge, Mass: Harvard University Press, 1940).
2. Edward H. Chamberlin, *The Theory of Monopolistic Competition*, 1st ed. (Cambridge, Mass: Harvard University Press, 1933); and 'Monopolistic Competition Revisited', *Economica*, November 1951.
3. Joan Robinson, *The Economics of Imperfect Competition*, 1st ed. (Macmillan, 1933) 4 and 307.
4. P. W. S. Andrews, 'Industrial Analysis in Economics with special reference to Marshall', in *Oxford Studies in the Price Mechanism*, ed. T. Wilson and P. W. S. Andrews (Oxford: Clarendon Press, 1951) 168.
5. If anyone has made the distinction before, in the way that I am making it, I apologise to him, but I have not been able to find it. Standard textbooks which I have consulted give a definition of 'industry' and 'market' (if they define these at all) in terms which are virtually interchangeable. When one goes to authors concerned with empirical data, one finds the same confusion. To take as an example *Dialogue on Concentration, Oligopoly and Profit: Concepts vs. Data* by Betty Bock (a Research Report from the Conference Board, 1972), she has put succinctly the problem of the Bureau of the Census definition of an industry:
   > Industry categories are slotted into the SIC system at the 4-digit level — which may, or may not, correspond to a trade definition. This is so because 4-digit Census industries are not defined according to a standard set of criteria. A 4-digit industry can be a relatively narrow category, such as 'malt', or a relatively broad category such as 'engineering and scientific instruments'. Some 4-digit industries represent categories where likeness of material is significant, such as 'asbestos products'; others represent categories

where likeness in use is significant, such as 'house slippers'; while others represent categories where likeness in distribution is important, as in 'pharmaceutical preparations'; and so on. (pp. 12–13)

The same problems arise with the British Census of Manufactures. The rest of the book makes it clear that Dr Bock, as an economist, would like to assimilate the definition of 'industry' to that of 'market'. Thus to the question 'Do standard industry concentration ratios have clear economic significance?' the answer is that it depends 'first, upon whether the Standard Industrial Classification system definition of the indstry corresponds to a competitive market'; and the example given is ' "paper towels" do not really compete with "toilet paper", although both are part of the 4-digit industry designated by the Bureau of the Census as "sanitary paper products" ' (p. 15) To the question 'What are the principal tests for determining whether a standard industry concentration ratio fits the competitive market to which it is related?' the first test given is 'Does the 4-digit industry represent a product, or group of products, surrounded by a gap in the chain of substitutes.' (p. 18) In other words, Dr Bock takes the economic definition of an industry to run in terms of a market, the boundaries of which are delineated by consumer preference. The same confusion is shown in the definition of oligopoly (p. 26). I repeat that I am keeping separate the concepts of industry and market, that industry is defined with reference to the supply side, and oligopoly refers to an industry with few producers. (Thus, I would say that paper towels and toilet paper are different *markets* but produced by firms in the same *industry*; and if we are concerned with producer-competition it is the latter concept which is the more relevant.

6. Alternatively, it could be considered as one industry in two sections, with a discontinuity in the cost curves.

7. Both quotations are from J. K. Galbraith, *American Capitalism*, rev. ed. (Boston: Houghton Mifflin, 1956) Chapter 9 'The Theory of Countervailing Power', 113–4.

8. J. S. Bain, *Barriers to New Competition* (Cambridge, Mass: Harvard University Press, 1956) 5 and *passim*.

9. See William H. Martin, 'Potential Competition and the United States Chlorine–Alkali Industry'; and Elizabeth Brunner 'A Note on Potential Competition'; both in *Journal of Industrial Economics*, July 1961.

10. For Andrews's theory of normal costs (which is taken for granted here) see his *Manufacturing Business*, 1st ed. (Macmillan, 1949), 'Industrial Analysis in Economics with special reference to Marshall', *op. cit.*, or Chapter 2 above.

11. In the original Hall and Hitch article ('Price Policy and Business Behaviour' *Oxford Economic Papers*, May 1939) which reported the costing-up process of arriving at price, which has been misinterpreted so often as 'full-cost' pricing, the evidence of the cotton firms shows that they were charging overheads on a 'standard' output basis; since their output was below that, they were in fact charging less than their full costs, in response, in this case, to the competition of cheap imports.

12. E.g. Smith's Potato Crisps. See 'The U.K. Potato Crisp Industry, 1960–72; a Study of New Entry Competition' by Alan Bevan, *Journal of Industrial Economics*, June 1974.

13. E.g. Associated Electrical Industries Ltd.

14. Cf. Joel Dean 'Pricing Pioneering Products', *Journal of Industrial Economics*, July 1969, where he discusses the different policies of 'skimming' or 'penetration' pricing.

Even when a monopoly is officially granted by a patent, firms are not completely independent of potential competitors in their price policy. If they put the price too high, others will come in, risking action for infringement of patent (cf. the classic case of the Biro pen) or designing round the patent.

15. An industry which is capital-intensive is likely to have considerable economies of scale, and therefore firms of a larger size, than a less capital-intensive industry. But, paradoxically, just because of these heavy capital costs there may be greater *disparities* of size among firms existing at any one time within such an industry than in a labour-intensive industry, because the less efficient firms there will have a lower proportion of paying-out costs than in a labour-intensive industry, and so will be harder to drive out.

16. We may illustrate the argument diagramatically:

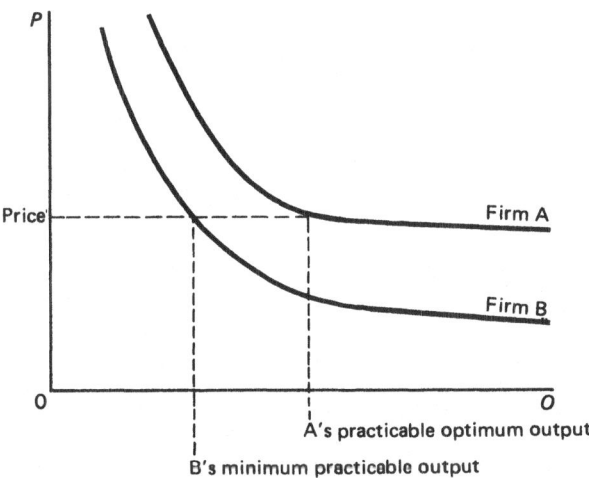

CHAPTER 4

1. The proceedings are reported in the following Law Reports: (1959) L.R. 1 R.P. 285; (1959) 1 W.L.R. 1118; (1959) 3 All E.R. 257. References in the text to the judgment are to the report in the *Reports of Restrictive Practices Cases*, Vol. 1, Part 6 (i.e. L.R. 1 R.P. 285–386).

2. See, for example, R. B. Stevens and B. S. Yamey, *The Restrictive Practices Court* (Weidenfeld and Nicolson, 1965) 194–200, or Yamey's earlier note 'In re Water-tube Boilermakers: contradictions and a paradox', *Modern Law Review*, January 1960.

3. E.g. A. Beacham 'Some Thoughts on the Cement Judgment', *Economic Journal*, 1962, and 'Some Further Thoughts on the Cement Judgment' I by J. B. Heath and II by J. R. Gould, *Economic Journal*, 1963; A. Sutherland 'Are Books Different?' *The Solicitor*, 1963; G. D. N. Worswick 'On the Benefits of being Denied the Opportunity to "Go Shopping" ' (on bolts and nuts), *Bulletin of the Oxford University Institute of Statistics*, 1961. Stevens and Yamey, *op. cit.*, go through each of the cases approved by the Court and criticise the Judgment in each one.

4. Perhaps I may illustrate the difference in approach by citing the form of legal argument: 'First, he did not do it; secondly, and nevertheless, if he did, he was justified in doing it.' This form of arguing, while perfectly possible for a lawyer, would not be possible for an economist.

5. C.f. R. B. Stevens and B. S. Yamey, *op. cit.*, 23–50.

6. The figures for the first three years were obtained from the *Central Electricity Report and Accounts*, annually. The series thereafter was constructed by taking the base figure, adding C.E. figures for boilers 'planned' and subtracting C.E.

figures for boilers commissioned. The work on this should largely be credited to Mr D. A. Grant (now Judge Grant Q.C.), junior counsel for the respondents.

7. The quotation is from the *Proceedings of the Sixth Electrical Power Convention*, Eastbourne, 1954, and the context is that Lord Citrine was asked to say something about the Monopolies and Restrictive Trade Practices Commission 'from the buyer's point of view'.

8. Ref. C.E.A. *Report and Accounts*, 1947–9, paras 173, 177.

9. Ref. C.E. *Report and Accounts*, 1957–8, para. 106.

10. *Report* of the Committee of Inquiry into Economy in the Construction of Power Stations (Beaver Committee), para. 2.

11. The C.E.A. had tried to get special prices from the Group concerned without success, and 'the suggestion was made that we should try and see if one manufacturer would break away on his own, and this was the result'. (Para. 237 of the Monopolies Commission's *Report on the Supply . . . of Electrical Machinery and Plant*; see also Chapter 9, section (3) generally.)

12. This figure is made up of £43 million, where the 'order values' of the contracts are definitely known to the Association, and of £8½ million, for which 'tabled values' have been taken as the best available approximation to order values.

CHAPTER 5

1. The present report does not discuss suggestions for future research which have come out of this inquiry, although all headings of the agenda produced valuable ideas for B.R.S. to consider.

2. Since a general undertaking prevents naming those concerned, this paper must be seen as implicit thanks for the great help which the invited businessmen gave to the seminar. Mention should also be made of one other business selected by Andrews and Brunner and visited by them at the first drafting stage so that their understanding of certain estimating and tendering procedures might be checked at that time.

3. Thus, for example, not all building firms are engaged in competitive tenders, and for most firms only a proportion of their activity will arise from such tenders, but the general effects of competitive tendering is an important matter because such tendering is in the aggregate a major area of building activity. To analyse the effects of tender competition in the selected features of the situation of a building firm will facilitate the assessment, not only of the implications for individual business but also for the industry as a whole, and so as a general economic-social factor. The value of such discussion for all those concerned with the building industry is not diminished because it is unaccompanied by statistical work; more theoretical work of this kind is a prerequisite for the improvement of statistical work on the industry and the sharpening of its relevance for the discussion of questions of public policy.

4. Of course, the fortunes of building-supply industries will be closely bound up with building activity and so with the building industry proper. In general economic history, in national planning, and so on, where we are concerned with industrial aggregates as we find them in practice, there may therefore be good reason to consider building together with such related activity; but it will be not the less important to keep in mind the elements of the whole complex which are distinctive for economic analysis.

5. This is important for any detailed discussion of the British industry, and particularly when making international comparisons, but it is one which we do not especially discuss in the present report.

6. Ref. P. W. S. Andrews, *On Competition in Economic Theory*, and especially pp. 57 and 78. (Note: Andrews uses the term cross-entry to cover *both* the entrance to this industry of a firm already established in another industry, *and* the entrance to a particular sub-market of a firm already in the same broad

'industry'. It is this latter concept which is particularly relevant here. In teaching we have found it necessary to coin the phrase 'within-entry' to distinguish this class from 'cross-entry' in the first sense.)

7. Because the qualities for actual success are to be tested only in the venture itself, because it may be relatively easy to start, on the basis of present opportunity, on a capital which is in fact small for continuance at that scale while dependent on successful competition for new business at the next stage, and above all because of the special risks of the uncertainties inherent in the building industry, easy entry conditions may well encourage more to chance their arm than will gain longer-term success. We may note that easy-entry are also easy-exit conditions, and building is known for the number of its bankruptcies, especially in the smaller-firm sectors. But this does not affect the economic thrust of competition from those in the industry at any one time, rather will that be accentuated by the competition of firms which are not securely lodged; see also following note. (We may add the comment, on the basis of the seminar's inquiry, that when thinking of failures, one must not overlook that the disappointed or failed entrepreneur may have another significance in this industry. We have referred already to the difficulties in finding, and therefore presently in training, intermediate management; one witness to the seminar remarked that failed builders were some of the most valuable recruits as foremen or site managers, their unlucky experience being a valuable kind of training for work at this important level in larger firms.)

8. This paragraph is a simple statement of a matter which has its pitfalls; in particular, to keep supply facilities in being does *not* entail, as usual theoretical statements would have it, that prices must be at a level which would cover the costs of all businesses. The facilities of less efficient businesses, as they are driven out through not covering minimum current costs may well be replaced by those of hopeful newcomers, when entry conditions are 'easy', as we argue to be the case in building in general. (See *On Competition in Economic Theory*, pp. 108–9 and 136.) For shorter periods of time, and as a general rule, prices will at least have to match the earning power elsewhere of financial and human resources which could be more rapidly withdrawn from the industry; it follows that periods of depression, with prices below long-term norms, may increase future supply difficulties through adverse effects on continuing organisation and facilities.

9. The term 'nuclear organisation', which we first hit on to denote this important factor in business strategy, was given up because of the possibility of confusion in a discussion of building, where the term may be used for special organisations which large firms have set up for nuclear-energy work.

10. A major reason for this treatment of labour may be that, although discussing the effects of specified changes of output, etc., traditional analysis has not paid enough attention to the general flux of the real business situation (apart from allowances for 'uncertainty' which do not meet the point now at issue); this means that in practice a businessman has to plan to produce efficiently a *range* of possible output, not just a given point of output per unit of time.

11. Ref. P. W. S. Andrews, *Manufacturing Business*, pp. 49, 96–7.

12. Broadly, current values are the 'opportunity costs' of economics which make most sense in competitive business problems, as businessmen themselves recognise in their 'costings', as distinct from accounts where historical values may have to be used.

13. On the managerial provision for fluctuations in outputs, as a matter applying more generally to manufacturing industry than orthodox theoretical models allow, see *Manufacturing Business*, pp. 87–99.

14. However, the simple generalisation, that average direct costs will be relatively constant for increased output of the same specification, is not valueless as

explaining the use of averages based on past experience in the costing of building projects for pricing purposes. Although this point is clearly of more general significance, in order to save repetition we discuss such 'costings' in the next section, 'The pricing of building works', with special reference to tenders.

15. For the very large business, able — in good times at least — to raise permanent finance by a stock-exchange issue, etc., one of the advantages of size is that it need not depend, for growth, so much on short-term finance and so will be the less vulnerable to short-term set-backs.

16. The reservation has reference to the fact that actual costs, as recorded by businesses, will have systematic differences due to (i) the fact that actual accounts have historical, and therefore peculiar, non-standard, elements, (ii) the effects of policy, in effect with regard to the disposal of available income, which happens to show itself in 'costs' — for example, expenditure on labour amenities. Although different in kind, so long as they are systematic these differences may be treated in the same way as 'real' cost differences.

17. In technical terms, our attitude is that, granted that this is a competitive industry in the sense which has been explained, and without making the atomistic equilibrium assumptions of orthodox competition theory, such stable cost differences may be dealt with on the lines of classical analysis as 'rents' which, although they may affect 'costing' calculations, will not affect the levels of prices which will be reached as a normal, long-run matter. The difference between our view and the classical, orthodox approach is that, as indicated in note 8, it is not assumed that 'marginal' firms will cover their costs at ruling prices, or that they will have to cover them to ensure long-term stability of supply (which we interpret as the maintenance of competitive capacity). Just holding on, their expectations (or the expectations of the new entrants who may take their places) will be based on intramarginal conditions. In effect, an analysis which recognises this may predicate lower normal levels of prices than will one which is based on atomistic equilibrium postulates.

18. One need not leap to suspicions of a preference for collusion — open or tacit — rather than competion, between businesses that 'know' one another. The costs of preparing bids can be extremely heavy and, having to do the work necessary to make a serious bid oneself, one may reasonably wish to have a fair chance against equally 'reasonable' competitors.

19. This is of course to disregard the complicating possibility that speculative buildings may be varied in detail at the finishing stage, to suit individual customers as they come along, even if variations are only by way of choice between preset alternatives.

20. More, the alleged advantages of negotiated contracts can be relied on by the customer only against the background of normal market prices which the existence of the competitive tender system will give both customers and advisers (and indeed the negotiating builders).

21. It is also somewhat illusory from the point of view of a guide to working costs as distinct from prices. It is for this reason that much research, notably at the Building Research Station, has gone into the development of 'operational bills' in which estimates for tender are analysed according to actual building operations rather than by elements of the finished building, in a form suitable for subsequent control of the work within the framework of the tender, and for the appreciation of the effects of practical variances on costs. One of the difficulties in this work has arisen from the very fact that traditional bills are designed for pricing and not for control purposes, and special procedures and considerable actual experience of them may be needed for the smooth use of operational bills as part of the tendering process. In so far as special work would have to be done before tender, which would not directly facilitate pricing as distinct from estimating operational costs when the work is proceeding, the new system would

also add to the overhead costs which, as we have seen, result from a builder having to tender for a number of contracts for every one in which he succeeds. It may be that the benefits to clients should lead to some formal allowance for such costs in some way or another. On the other hand, of course, a good deal of the impetus towards operational bills comes from the fact that much work has to be done for tender with traditional b.o.q.'s which could be made useful for later management by operational bills but which is at present virtually wasted.

22. In the sense of expenses incurred, or estimated to be incurred, by reason of productive activity, when fairly allocated under appropriate accounting headings to particular periods and products.

23. In the sense of figures whose purpose is to relate details of production to current factor prices in such a way as to link presently contemplated products to previous products, so that earlier experience of market-price/cost relationships may be used as a guide to presently available prices.

24. This adjustment of costings to meet market conditions is clearly a distinct matter from the adjustment of overall margin on account of particular desire on the part of the business to get a contract with a certain operational make-up, already referred to, though a *common* adjustment of tender margins of this kind will produce the changes in effective market prices which are sufficiently common to have to be reckoned in costings.

25. For this paragraph we are indebted to a memorandum by Mr John Flemming.

# Index